Originally established by the Nuffield Foundation in 1975, the **Centre for Agricultural Strategy** is a self-financing unit within the Faculty of Agriculture and Food at the University of Reading.

Contents

Acknowledgements

The Centre gratefully acknowledges the support and advice provided by the following organisations:

 The European Commission

 Allied Grain Group

 J Bibby Agriculture

 Cargill Europe

 Ciba Agriculture

 Dalgety Agriculture

 Dow Elanco Europe

 Hydro Agri (UK)

 John Deere

 Kemira Ince

 Massey Ferguson (United Kingdom)

 Plant Breeding International Cambridge

ZENECA Zeneca Agrochemicals

7

Abbreviations and Acronyms

ACP	Africa, the Caribbean and the Pacific
ADAS	Agricultural Development and Advisory Service
CAP	Common Agricultural Policy
CAS	Centre for Agricultural Strategy
CEE	Central and Eastern Europe
CEEC	Central and Eastern European Countries
CFP	Common Fisheries Policy
°C	°Celsius
CIMMYT	International Maize and Wheat Improvement Center
CLA	Country Landowners' Association
COMECON	Council for Mutual Economic Assistance
DDT	Dichlorodiphenyltrichloroethane
DG II	Directorate for Economic and Financial Affairs
DG VI	Directorate for Agriculture
DME	Developed Market Economies
ECU	European Currency Unit
EFTA	European Free Trade Association
ETSU	Energy Technology Support Unit
ESAs	Environmentally Sensitive Areas
EU	European Union
FAO	Food and Agriculture Organisation of the United Nations
f.o.b.	free on board
FWAG	Farming and Wildlife Advisory Group
GATT	General Agreement on Tariffs and Trade
GDP	Gross Domestic Product
ha	hectare
HMSO	Her Majesty's Stationery Office
IFPRI	International Food Policy Research Institute
km	kilometre
lb	pound (weight)
LDCs	Less Developed Countries
kwh	kilowatt hour
MAFF	Ministry of Agriculture, Fisheries and Food
MDCs	More Developed Countries
MLC	Meat and Livestock Commission
MP	Member of Parliament
Mt	Megatonne (s)
NFU	National Farmers' Union
NSAs	Nitrate Sensitive Areas
OECD	Organisation for Economic Co-operation and Development

p	pence
REAG	Renewable Energy Advisory Group
RUNS	Rural-Urban North-South
SAFE	Sustainable Agriculture, Food and Environment
SSSIs	Sites of Special Scientific Interest
UAE	United Arab Emirates
UR	Uruguay Round
UK	United Kingdom
UKASTA	United Kingdom Agricultural Supply Trade Association
UNEP	United Nations Environment Programme
US	United States
USDA	United States Department of Agriculture
USSR	Union of Soviet Socialist Republics
WWF	Worldwide Fund for Nature
WTO	World Trade Organisation

Professor John Marsh, CBE,
Director, Centre for Agricultural Strategy
welcomes
The Rt Hon William Waldegrave, MP,
Minister of Agriculture, Fisheries and Food

Preface

The major reforms of the Common Agricultural Policy agreed in 1992, the 1993 GATT settlement, the accession of three countries to the European Union on 1st January 1995, and its possible extension in the longer term to several central and eastern European countries, present a daunting array of uncertainties. These affect not only farmers, but all those industries concerned with the supply of farm inputs and the processing and marketing of farm outputs. The present delicately balanced deal in relation to agricultural policy and trade will almost certainly come under increasing pressure.

The purpose of this conference was to confront the implications of these developments and to debate what sorts of strategies and policy options may be possible. To do so it brought together experts in the fields involved. To encourage the fullest possible analysis of the issues and uninhibited debate, the conference was organised in three parts. Firstly, four key papers addressed likely global food requirements into the next century and the challenges and opportunities this presents for European agriculture. The issues covered included the likely effect of the Uruguay Round Agreement, the linkages between agricultural and environmental policies and the medium term outlook for the CAP in the context of trends in international trade. Secondly, representatives of the production, agricultural supply and marketing, and agrochemicals sections of the industry responded. They focused on practical aspects, the problems of planning their businesses, of determining the nature and direction of research and their view on the strategies and policies that need to be in place to enable them to meet these challenges successfully. The final group of papers provided an informed analysis of the main policy issues. These include price and income support, decoupling, supply control, structural policies, rural development and costs falling on the EU budget. They also offered pointers to possible ways in which policies could be reordered to reflect the new agricultural and environmental priorities. The conference closed with a brief summary and some conclusions drawn from the day's proceedings.

The publication of these proceedings will take forward in a co-ordinated way, the well-informed material and views that were presented and debated. Together with the conclusions and recommendations of studies by the National Farmers' Union, the Country Landowners' Association and the European Programme of The Royal Institute of International Affairs they will enrich the policy making process. The intention of the Ministry of Agriculture, Fisheries and Food and the Department of the Environment to issue a joint White Paper on the future of our rural areas later this year makes evident the timely nature of the debate. CAS is grateful to all who took part and supported this meeting, and for the opportunity to make a contribution to the development of these ideas.

J S Marsh
Director
Centre for Agricultural Strategy

Marshall BJ & Miller FA (Eds)(1995) *Priorities for a new century - agriculture, food and rural policies in the European Union*. CAS Paper 31. Reading: Centre for Agricultural Strategy.

Address - Pressures on the CAP

The Rt Hon William Waldegrave, MP

INTRODUCTION

I am delighted to be here in such a distinguished gathering of experts on the Common Agricultural Policy (CAP). After four months in the job and three Agriculture Councils, I am far from being an expert. The trouble is I sometimes suspect that the CAP, with its relation the Common Fisheries Policy (CFP), is so complicated and takes such an effort to understand, that those who do understand it fully are inclined to protect their investment by resisting further change! But reading the programme for today's conference it seems that there is beginning to be an underlying assumption in the United Kingdom (UK) at least that the CAP must change - and that is surely right. It is impossible to think of the European Union (EU) moving into the next century with today's policies which in large measure still reflect the priorities of the 1950s and 1960s. Encouragingly that is not now just a British view. European farming has changed dramatically over the last three decades and it will continue to develop rapidly in the next. It falls to the politicians to ensure that the right policies are in place to assist that development.

CAS is to be congratulated on an extremely well-balanced programme, covering the range of issues which farmers, their leaders and politicians need to address. I should like to focus on where I, as a politician, see the pressures for change coming. The CAP has shown itself uniquely resistant to change over the years. There is massive inertia to be overcome. So it is vital to understand from where the pressures for change will come. Only then can we build a strategy to ensure that those changes are the right ones.

13

It is as well to be clear about one thing. The EU and the UK within it, need to have a common agricultural policy. The British food and farming industries benefit enormously from the single European market, of which a common policy for agriculture is a vital part. Our food, feed and drinks exports to the single market area in the first 6 months of this year rose by £391.7 million compared with the first six months of 1992. Some sectors have achieved spectacular success - for example, sheepmeat exports rose by 177% and beef exports by 100%. Renationalising the CAP means nothing if it means competitive subsidy and renewed barriers to trade. I want to see a common European framework within which British agriculture - and European agriculture - can take on the world in fair competition. That is the goal we seek to achieve. We will succeed only if we - as a Union - understand the pressures and find the right responses. Those pressures come from the international community. They come from the market place and from the public whose support for agriculture is essential to its future. And they come from the Union's own intentions for its future size and scope, and the practical consequences which flow from those intentions. I shall look at these pressures in turn.

GENERAL AGREEMENT ON TARIFFS AND TRADE (GATT)

First, the international community. The completion of the Uruguay Round one year ago was a major achievement which looked like it might never happen. Failure to agree would have been disastrous for the EU, entailing the risk of a general trade war and reopening highly damaging legal challenges to the CAP. The Peace Clause, which formed part of the agreement, protects the CAP from challenge for nine years. Most importantly, the GATT agreement set the CAP on an inexorable new course - in the direction of the market. Firstly, because GATT provided the catalyst for the 1992 CAP reforms, the EU made an important shift away from price support, through the significant cuts in prices for cereals and beef, and towards supporting farmers by direct payments; and secondly, because the reductions in support are now embodied in legally binding commitments on internal support, subsidised exports, and market access laid down in GATT. These apply until 2000 and beyond if no successor agreement has been reached. And the Peace Clause only remains valid if CAP support for individual sectors does not exceed that decided in 1992. So there are real constraints on the market support provided by the CAP. And the clear intention when the new round of GATT negotiations opens in 1999 is that those commitments will be taken further. Thirdly, the GATT agreement has given an important boost to world trade, opening up new markets and creating new opportunities. Agricultural industries around the world must now respond to this and it is the efficient who will be best able to compete. So it must be in the interests of the Community to ensure that its efficient farmers are able to exploit their advantages internationally. That means not imposing unnecessary costs on businesses or hampering their ability to respond flexibly to the market with supply controls. And it means not importing into policy a bias against holdings of an efficient size. This all points to a CAP under pressure to move closer to the market.

CONSUMER AND TAXPAYER PRESSURES

Pressures from consumers and taxpayers are also pointing in the same direction. The shift to supporting farmers through direct payments has, paradoxically, made the diminished amount of subsidy being spent on agriculture much more transparent. To a much greater extent, support now falls on farmers' doormats in the form of large cheques and is not routed through millions of consumer transactions. Many farmers themselves feel rather uneasy about this. And not surprisingly, the general public want to know why farmers should receive these handouts when other, in their eyes equally deserving, sectors of industry do not. In other member states where subsidising certain parts of industry comes perhaps more naturally, there is less outrage. But even there, questions are now beginning to be asked. The public might accept the large transfers more readily if they felt it was the price they had to pay for cheap food. But they know that even now, after the 1992 reforms, the CAP still keeps food prices too high. It is easy to criticise the figures produced by the Organisation for Economic Co-operation and Development (OECD) which suggest that the CAP costs the average family of four £20 per week. We all know that if the CAP did not exist, world prices would not be so depressed and that these figures therefore exaggerate the real cost to consumers. But that does not change the fact that consumers are paying an unacceptably high price and they know it. So pressures from the public are increasing because they know that the CAP costs them too much. The all-too-frequent stories about CAP fraud only exacerbate the public's doubts.

CONSUMER CHOICE

Just as important a pressure comes from changing consumer demand. In an affluent society, with a decreasing proportion of household expenditure spent on food, consumers demand choice and variety. They demand new products, and new uses of traditional products. It is no longer enough for agriculture simply to produce bulk commodities without any regard for the market. The agriculture and food industries must respond to demand. They must tailor production to the consumers' needs. They can only do that if they are responsive to the market. That means they need clear signals from the market. We policymakers must ensure that we avoid policies which interfere with these signals and encourage farmers to produce something other than what their customers want. Our food processing industry in the EU, and particularly here in the UK, is amongst the most dynamic in the world. It is our farmers' principal customer. If we go on forcing our food processors to pay high prices for their raw materials, or limiting their supply through quotas, or depriving them of the quality of product they need, we should not be surprised if the investment goes elsewhere. And that means loss of jobs. In the interest of the European economy as a whole - but no less in the interests of our farmers - our agricultural policy must create the conditions in which our food industry can prosper.

ENVIRONMENTAL AND WELFARE PRESSURES

But the pressures on the CAP are not just economic. Here and elsewhere, the public demand that agricultural policy should also take account of the environment. The UK has been at the forefront of the pressure for change in the CAP to make it more environmentally friendly. I certainly intend to continue that. But despite our successes, such as the agri-environment programme, there is still only 1% of the CAP budget spent on environmental schemes. The main problem of the CAP for the environment comes back to the central issue - that levels of support have been too high. So farmers have had economic incentives over many years to intensify production, with familiar consequences - loss of habitats, pollution and landscape change. One response to this problem is by building environmental considerations into CAP support arrangements. Incentives to manage the land in particular environmentally-friendly ways are another. But the single most important change we could achieve for the benefit of the environment would be to reduce the levels of market distorting support. This would encourage farming at a lower level of intensity, with fewer inputs. And it might enable us to redirect some of the resources swallowed up by the CAP towards positive environmental ends.

As well as having one of the most vocal environmental lobbies, we in the UK also have the most active animal welfare lobby. That is no bad thing. It is not acceptable for animals to be treated inhumanely and, as all good farmers know, it does not make economic sense either. But there is no doubt that the massive media and public interest here in the whole issue of animal welfare ensures that farming remains in the spotlight, and can only increase the pressure on the CAP.

CENTRAL AND EASTERN EUROPE (CEE) ENLARGEMENT

But perhaps the most important pressure on the CAP comes from the Union's own vision of its future - and in particular from its plans to expand eastwards to embrace the former Communist countries of central and eastern Europe. This is the major challenge now facing the Union. Enlarging the EU to the East is the best guarantee of future democracy and stability in Europe. It is of fundamental importance to Europe's future. No-one is under any illusion that it will be easy. There is massive development and restructuring to be done in the CEE countries first and the EU itself must also adapt if it is to make the transition to a Community of twenty or more member states. This is true in many areas, but particularly so for agriculture.

Western European agriculture would face many challenges in adapting to a single market stretching from the Atlantic to the borders of Russia and the Ukraine. The CEE countries have enormous potential to increase their output of agricultural products directly competing with those of the current EU. The Union's farmers will need to prepare themselves for the extra competition from this production, as well as for the opportunities which the new CEE markets will create. They will not want to be shackled by a high cost base, output quotas or an outdated and inefficient farm structure. It cannot moreover make sense to spend Western taxpayers' money encouraging CEE producers to expand their production beyond that which is economically justified only to exacerbate the problems. But that is what applying to them the mechanisms of the present CAP - as some have suggested - would mean. In addition, the surpluses which would result from applying the present CAP to the CEE countries would put unbearable pressure on the Union's budget. And extending support at current high levels to CEE production would be incompatible with the Union's commitments under the GATT. It is of course inconceivable that fundamentally different support regimes could apply to the CEE countries, once they become Union members, at least for very long. The CAP itself will therefore need to be adapted to ensure EU enlargement can take place without these adverse effects. Enlargement to the East is an unprecedented opportunity for the EU which it cannot afford to miss. But for the reasons I have spelt out it also makes further CAP reform a necessity. As the Prime Minister has already made clear, it must be a root and branch reform. We need to establish the right framework for a CAP which would be appropriate to the needs of an enlarged EU. The pressures are compelling. And the *status quo* is not an option. We shall need to make those changes before the CEE countries are admitted to full membership. And as I have made clear, there is only one way forward - towards the market. Building protectionist walls and insulating our farmers from ever-changing market forces by quotas, Set-aside and other supply controls cannot be realistic options for the 21st century.

CONCLUSION

How will we get there? There is no easy route - if there were, we would already have followed it. There will be obstacles on the way, and some reluctant travellers. We cannot ignore farmers' very real anxieties about what they see as perpetual change. But ignoring the pressures is not an option. We need to be clear about what policy framework will best enable European farming to respond to the pressures, and then to work hard to achieve it. I do not have a blueprint solution. But equally, I would be failing British farmers and the public if I did not do my best to define a clear vision for the future. It was in order to help me achieve this that I announced, last month, my intention to set up a CAP policy group which I shall chair. I want to bring together a small team of independent thinkers to pool their experience and brainstorm ideas about the future of the CAP. I do not intend to create a new bureaucracy, so the team will be small and its members will be invited to join in a personal capacity and not as representatives of any sector or interest group. It will include academics, businessmen and farming practitioners. The group will focus on real, practical ideas which can be negotiated with our partners, and not on theories which have no application in the real world. I hope to be able to announce the names of the participants shortly.

Chairman, this is an important conference looking at key issues for the future of European agriculture. The challenges which farming has to face as we move towards the next century are profound. But I know that farmers in this country in particular are willing to take them on constructively and creatively. I, as Minister of Agriculture, will do everything in my power to facilitate that. I certainly intend to make my contribution to setting the priorities for a New Century in agricultural policies in the EU.

DISCUSSION

Mr J Brady (National Farmers' Union of Scotland) said that whereas the previous Minister of Agriculture, Fisheries and Food had indicated on return from Brussels three years ago that the new CAP reforms were a triumph for the Government, the Minister in his current address had implied that they were a bad deal for farmers and consumers.

Mr Anthony Bosanquet (Country Landowners' Association) also referred to differences of approach to CAP reforms (between the Agricultural Commissioner and the UK Minister) and stressed the importance of persuading European agricultural colleagues that significant problems remain to be addressed.

Mr Waldegrave in reply commented that the MacSharry reforms were the outcome of a complex and arduous round of negotiations which were rightly applauded by the NFU, especially in relation to the resistance of pressures to bias agricultural policies against the farm size structure in the UK. He considered that the reforms had worked better than predicted in bringing down production surpluses and in restraining budgetary expenditure, but in view of the further implications of the GATT settlement, the enlargement of the EU, and changing consumer demands, the Council of Agricultural Ministers do recognise that reform is by no means at an end and further issues and problems must be confronted. He recognised, however, that whilst a huge job of attitudinal change lies ahead, movement in the right direction is detectable.

Ms Vicki Hird (Sustainable Agriculture, Food and Environment Alliance) (SAFE) welcomed the Minister's comments on the need for further reform of the CAP and asked him to stress at meetings on the CAP and the World Trade Organisation (WTO), the need for adequate impact assessments, in relation to both environmental and social policies and mechanisms set up by the EU, in order to ensure that other countries and people do not suffer as a result of our trade policies, for instance through subsidised exports. The Minister was also asked to comment on the role of the large UK retailers, their often damaging control over the production activities of farmers and growers, and the need for some policy control of their power and dominance over the regional marketplaces.

Mr Waldegrave's view was that contrary to arguments made by the environmental movement, GATT is a beneficial development for Third World agricultural producers because if we can limit subsidised exports, then producers have greater incentives and opportunities to build up their own farming businesses. On the question of the influence of retailers on the producers and processors of food, Mr Waldegrave considered that the supermarkets exercise beneficial effects by working with them to raise the quality of products and provide significant marketing opportunities both in the UK and in European countries where some larger supermarket companies have become established. Producers furthermore benefit from consumer preference for their products bearing supermarket brand names.

Sir Simon Gourlay referred to the Minister's statement that only 1% of the CAP budget is currently spent on environmental schemes, and invited him to speculate on what would be a realistic percentage figure for future expenditure on environmental and structural measures.

Mr Waldegrave felt unable to propose any precise figure but referred in more general terms to the arguments for and against the allocation of funds for 'dual agricultural/environmental' practices. He considered that such an approach may require excessive levels of inspection and monitoring and accordingly advocated working towards a more realistic supply, demand and pricing regime that would be less likely to create pressure for removal of hedgerows and habitats, and cropping of areas of upland, thus resulting in a natural process of restoration of the agricultural and environmental balance.

Marshall BJ & Miller FA (Eds)(1995) *Priorities for a new century - agriculture, food and rural policies in the European Union.* CAS Paper 31. Reading: Centre for Agricultural Strategy.

1 Food and agriculture: a global perspective

Jock R Anderson

INTRODUCTION

I really welcome this opportunity to ponder a global perspective for food and agriculture on my favourite planet, not least because it is in line with our decisions to gather here today: we are all inescapably interested in this topic that has such weighty consequences, for not only our own future ken, but for our species and its welfare. Naturally, however, our individual perspectives on the topic vary greatly, reflecting not only its inherent complexity but the diversity in our individual perceptions.

I come to today's topic largely from the experience in and information gleaned from several years in the World Bank's central Agriculture and Natural Resources Department, and a rather lengthy period of active involvement with the International Agricultural Research Centers of the Consultative Group on International Agricultural Research. You will form your own opinion of where I sit in the optimistic-pessimistic alarmist-complacent spectra, but I will strive to be realistic, while alerting you to some critical conditions necessary for underpinning and rationalising whatever optimism you find in my 'realism'.

My approach here is a simple one of sharing with you my own best judgment of the prospects for global food and agriculture, and of trying to present the situation in a form that does not imply an unjustifiable level of precision in projections that extend to a time when I will not be alive to defend them. The field is remarkably controversial, and another approach – one adopted just a month ago by my colleague Alex McCalla in his Crawford Lecture – would be to review critically the diverse positions that have recently been taken, from Mitchell & Ingco (1994) to Brown & Kane (1994), to mention just two rather extreme scenarios. Since McCalla has done this so ably, and as I have neither the time nor space to repeat the exercise, I present my simplified interpretation, comforted that my 'conditionally conventional' view happens to match that of McCalla fairly closely. In so saying, I should also share one of his pithy paragraphs (McCalla, 1994, p. 22):

'Of course, no one knows who will be right. Projections thirty years ahead, particularly those by economists, are invariably wrong. This is partly because of questionable assumptions, limited models, and poor information, but also because a dynamic world economy is self-adjusting since it does not tolerate disequilibrium easily.'

SOME DEFINING DIMENSIONS OF REALITY
Time
Naturally a first dimension is time. My temporal horizon is primarily to the next three decades or so, which will take us well into the (for us) most important portion of the 'new century,' and yet be close enough in time to permit me to put aside for the present purpose the many so far unresolvable uncertainties about the food and agricultural implications of the enhanced Greenhouse Effect and of policies that bear on its evolution: themes that doubtless will be taken up in many future conferences (Downing & Parry 1994; Norse, 1994).

Population
Yet this short period does offer challenge enough for contemplation, providing as it does for some impressive if not disturbing increases in global population, mostly in the presently less-developed countries (LDCs), as depicted by the projections summarised in Table 1.1.

Table 1.1
Human population (billion)

Country group	1995 (%)	2025 (%)
LDCs[a]	4.5	7.1
MDCs[b]	1.2	1.4
Total	5.7	8.5

[a] Less-developed countries
[b] More-developed countries
Source: United Nations (1993)

Food needs

Making detailed projections of the aggregate food needs for humanity is a task that involves the deployment of considerable information, much of which is even more speculative and uncertain than the analogous information on population levels to which they are applied. For an overview, however, the situation can be appreciated through constructing simplified scenarios focused on the major sources of food energy, namely, the cereals, and relating consumption patterns for 'average' consumers to plausible changes in average income levels across country groups. Such a process should, if done in a consistent and comprehensive way, also involve the modelling of the formation of market prices of all goods, including food products generally and major sources of food energy specifically, and the corresponding choices by consumers as prices and incomes vary over time. Such comprehensive studies are costly and are subject to inevitable controversy and uncertainty and thus, not surprisingly, are rare. To focus quickly on the Big Picture, I resort to one such simplified scenario assembly in which I have been involved (Crosson & Anderson 1992, 1994). Imagining what a megaton (Mt) of wheat 'looks like' is difficult enough, but the 3300 Mt (about 2.5 km³) of total cereal needs in 2030 (Table 1.2) is large indeed and, significantly, is nearly double the size of the cereal mountain 'consumed' in any recent year – the quotes reminding us that apparent consumption involves much apparent waste, as highlighted recently by Bender (1994).

Table 1.2
Food on the plate: 1990 and 2030

Country group/crop	Approximate 1990 (Mt)	Projected 2030 (Mt)	Implied average annual growth rate (%)	1980s historic rate (%)
LDCs				
Rice	310	640	1.8	2.6
Wheat	270	770	2.6	3.7
Coarse Grains	300	950	2.9	1.7
LDC total	880	2360	2.5	2.6
MDC total	800	940	0.4	-
World total	1680	3300	1.7	-

Source: Apparent aggregate cereal consumption, rounded and extracted from Crosson & Anderson (1992, p 12).

RESOURCES: DEGRADATION *v* SUSTENANCE

Many of the resources that support agriculture are limited in supply in various ways, such as having a sharply increasing cost per unit beyond some critical level. The critical level may be:

- essentially infinite, as is the case for most atmospheric gases;
- probably rather finite, as for, say, petroleum-based energy;
- slowly approached, as is the case for financial and capital resources;
- fairly clearly delineated, as is the case for agricultural land;
- potentially quite confining, such as water.

The list of resources is long and the constraints that may be associated with them diverse, especially in their local specificities. Generalisations thus run the danger of falsity, especially when applied to particular agricultural niches, but must be made in order to examine the likely form of the Big Picture.

The following sections focus on land, water and knowledge resources, all of which are 'human' resources, in the sense that they serve most productively when the property rights in them are clear, secure and hopefully fair. Depending in part on the nature of such property rights of individual farm managers, the discussion must also recognise the reality that a given resource can vary greatly in quality, over space and over time, often for the worse, in which case the situation may be described generically as resource degradation – encompassing such varied phenomena as desertification, erosion, salinisation, exhaustion, compaction, toxification, and so on.

Degradation is thus a phenomenon that has many manifestations, most of which are resource-specific. Land degradation is one of the most widely recognised forms, especially in its most dramatic form of gully soil erosion, rather less in more subtle forms such as dryland salinity buildup. But every resource is potentially susceptible to degradation and erosion. The knowledge resource itself, to which I return with some passion later, can also be degraded, as its structures of support decline (such as an absence of fresh 'injections' of human capital from cutting-edge post-graduate programmes; libraries and their users losing contact with contemporary thinking through non-renewal of journal subscriptions; an absence of current reference texts and ready international professional contacts; inadequate incentives to add productively to the knowledge store; under extreme conditions, the deliberate distortion of evidence, constituting scientific fraud).

Whether it be land, water or atmosphere, human capital, the knowledge resource or other perhaps even more fragile resources, the reality of degradation must be considered and allowed for in assessments of future resource situations. The possibilities are not always 'well balanced' in terms of symmetry but the obverse of degradation, enhancement of a resource, is in principle possible.

Enhancement sometimes may be costly but if the rewards are adequate, (which may require increased security of tenure in some resources such as land, and even life itself - some contemporary cases in sub-Saharan Africa do spring to mind), happen it will, with the consequent positive outcomes for boosted private returns and productivity.

The land resource
Measuring actual land use at a global level (FAO 1994) has its own subtleties that need not distract us today, but assessing future potential use is a real art form, fortunately tackled regularly by FAO, (see Table 1.3). Taking a stab at actual conversions to cropland by any designated future time goes beyond art and certainly beyond science – involving as it does judgments about many different societies' changing values of both the economic and environmental costs of changed land use – but this is done for the purpose of concreteness in the final column of Table 1.3.

Table 1.3
Cropland overview: recent and for the year 2030 (million ha)

Region	Cropped 1990	Technically arable but uncropped 1990	Guesstimated realistic new cropland to 2030[a]
sub-Saharan Africa	210	800	40
West Asia/ North America	80	10	5
East Asia	210	100	30
South Asia	190	40	20
Latin America/ Caribbean	190	870	50
LDCs	880	1820	145
MDCs	600	80	5
World	1480	1900	150

[a] Given needs for animal pastures and forests, infrastructural limitations, new urban land occupations, tsetse-related impediments to conversion, rising environmental opportunity costs and constraints arising from use of lower quality land.

Source: FAO (1994)

Adding an additional 150 million ha (about 10%) to the world's cropland over 40 years may seem modest enough relative to recent past-decade annual increments of the order of 1%, but even this, I think, will be difficult, infrastructurally demanding, and politically controversial in many (especially 'green') quarters. Whatever may, in fact, prove to be attainable, it seems to me – and here I am rather more pessimistic than is my colleague Pierre Crosson – that this source of meeting the 1.7 % annual growth challenge of Table 1.2 will in itself be minor (ie only about 0.25 %).

These overview remarks about land are simplistically quantitative and crude in that they take no account of qualitative dimensions, such as the diversity of land productivities (both in present and potential cropland), the extent and consequences of the many forms of land degradation and the effective-supply-increasing consequences of various land improvement interventions such as application of organic and inorganic fertilisers, terracing, tied ridging, 'conservation farming' methods such as zero tillage, and of land reclamation endeavours, expensive as these may sometimes be.

Space forbids an analysis of this controversial area here (much of the literature is critically examined by Crosson & Anderson, 1992 and Crosson 1994) but, on balance, and without considerable investment, such land-quality enhancement activities over the four decades may well outpace the new losses to degradation to the tune of another net 10% equivalent increase of the land resource, ie, about another 0.25 % per annum contribution to the needed 1.7 % annual increase in production.

Needless to say, what is actually achieved in the management of land will depend crucially on the policy environment that surrounds this most special of resources. Different cultures differ greatly in the way they approach the land resource, ranging from strong public ownership with little real security of individualised tenure in, say, parts of the former Soviet Union through to unconstrained privately owned and fully alienable land at the other extreme, with many intermediate gradations of ownership and thus of incentive for responsible custodial management. A favourable outcome by way of the enhanced productivity foreshadowed above will thus rely on a progressive evolution of tenurial incentives for individuals to manage their land with greater regard to the rights of future users.

The water resource
The next physical resource with which I must deal, if only briefly, is water, particularly in its role of irrigation for crops, although the scarcity issues to be touched on also link strongly to non-agricultural uses of water, such as the various human-driven imperative urban, industrial and domestic purposes, and less pressing but nonetheless significant recreational purposes.

The global situation for irrigated area can be viewed in a manner parallel to that for the land resource, of which it is of course a part, as is presented in Table 1.4. The numbers in Table 1.4 seem much smaller than those of Table 1.3 for several good reasons, notably that irrigation is quite an expensive practice and is becoming more so in several ways (Yudelman, 1994). First, many of the undeveloped projects have geomorphological and engineering attributes that make them as much as twice as expensive as earlier typical schemes, a situation exacerbated by high transport/transaction costs in more remote sites. Second, there is now growing recognition of the short-sightedness in inadequately dealing with drainage in many early schemes, and attention to this both retrospectively and prospectively 'increases' irrigation costs from their apparent to higher real levels. Third, and most significantly, the social and environmental costs, especially of large schemes in heavily populated possibly 'fragile' areas are being better recognised, more vehemently articulated, and more adequately taken into account. Such considerations explain the pessimism evident in the final-column guesstimates of Table 1.4.

Table 1.4
Irrigated land overview: recent and for 2030 (million ha)

Region	Irrigated[a] 1990	Technically potentially irrigable 1990	Guesstimated realistic new irrigated land
sub-Saharan Africa	4	16	4
West Asia/ North America	8	2	0
East Asia	140	60	20
South Asia	20	6	4
Latin America/ Caribbean	16	24	4
LDCs	188	108	32
MDCs	68	26	2
World	256	134	34

[a] Based on World Bank/UNDP (1990, p 115), rounded to the nearest even number.

The highor land productivity of irrigated agriculture relative to non-irrigated (an average yield factor of 2.5) must be recognised in assessing the guesstimated contribution of new irrigation investment to meeting the demand scenarios. Assuming the new irrigation is on existing cropland, the net increase in the total-productivity-equivalent land resource is some 50 million ha (on top of the 150) to 2030, which contributes only an additional 0.08 % per year.

Analogous to the case of land, however, there are qualitative aspects to consider, along with the sheer magnitudes of areas nominally irrigated. The productivity of this resource depends on several attributes such as timing of delivery relative to needs, requests and intentions, and reliability of supply generally, not to mention the quality (eg, salt, nutrients, silt and pesticide (Farah 1994) burdens) of the water itself. Most of the attributes can best be considered under the general heading of 'management,' a field presently handled inadequately in many irrigation schemes. With greater attention to overcoming wasteful and inefficient management practices through research, training, pricing and incentives, much may be achieved over the coming decades and, accordingly, I feel that progress here could be some 1.5 times as effective as new schemes themselves to the year 2030, bringing the total likely contribution of the water resource to $0.08 + 0.12 = 0.2$ % per year.

As is the case for the land resource, policy attitudes adopted towards the water resource will be of great consequence (World Bank, 1993). The ownership and user rights issues in water are, however, even more complicated than those for land and thus the opportunities for enhancing qualitative aspects of the water resource are not so favourable. This is not to say that governments should not address themselves vigorously to clarifying the rights of users of the water resource, especially as it becomes increasingly scarce over coming decades. They **must** address these issues, even though they involve conflicts – intranational and international – that are among the most difficult to resolve (Umali, 1993, Kirmani & Rangeley 1994).

With the important exception taken up in the next section, I feel it is unlikely that other biophysical resources (such as climate and plant and animal genetic resources *per se*) will play much of a role in identifying the production growth equation to the year 2030, so it is time to summarise the assessment thus far. It has been speculated that, of the needed annual average growth of 1.7% per annum, 0.5 will come from the land resource and 0.2 from the water resource, which leaves about 1 % per annum to be found elsewhere. I think this quest should lead us in the general direction of technology and knowledge.

The knowledge resource

The foregoing review of the limited prospects for the major physical resources leads to a direct consideration of the one resource that is not so limited or limiting, but yet requires rather special handling. Agricultural knowledge, as expressed in an efficiently productive agriculture, has many rather special features, which include (Francis 1990) being non-rival in use, readily expandable through appropriate investment, easily transmissible, and productively integrative.

The supply of new knowledge can be conceptualised usefully as being distributed among three major components: human capital, institutional innovation (including policy), and improved technology.

All three are vital and any sensible development strategy must address them all carefully. For brevity and also simplicity, since it is somewhat less difficult to measure, I will here focus on the technology leg of this stool.

To summarise a large and rich literature all too succinctly, investment in agricultural knowledge systems has generally (at least according to some 200 retrospective studies) proved to be highly socially rewarding, with internal rates of return usually in the region of 30% and with seemingly few total failures. This is not to suggest that every ECU (or whatever) invested in agricultural knowledge systems is necessarily well spent – more of this later, when I touch on some of the pressing needs in sub-Saharan Africa – but a socially responsible investment programme must be alert to both opportunities and challenges.

Fortunately, the reality of these diverse situations is increasingly well understood in the development community. Donors and recipients alike are becoming rather more discerning than has often been the case, when the needs perceived may have overwhelmed the realism of judgements that may have been driven more by donor priorities and 'needs' rather than the 'real' concerns of the people in recipient and beneficiary communities.

To return now to the demand scenario that remains unmet by increased land and water resources, can the 'missing' 1% per year be provided by conventional inputs and the knowledge resource? When Crosson & Anderson (1992) looked at this question, we decided it could – subject to the crucial proviso that investment in the new-technology generating systems (largely International Agricultural Research Centers and National Agricultural Research Systems) remains strong, stable and efficient. In the present era of diminished real resources for both international and national research, this too is indeed a further key issue that must remain on the policy agenda. Those concerned with public resource allocation must revisit the lowered priority implicitly assigned to research investment. With re-invigorated research resource commitments, however, significant productivity growth seems achievable, perhaps towards the speculative possibilities for land-productivity growth for some key crops depicted in Table 1.5.

As in the past (Byerlee, 1994), local achievements will vary greatly according to many local circumstances but, with aggregate performances in both (a) varietal improvement and (b) management (including fertiliser use), perhaps each of the order of the 0.8% per year indicated in Table 1.5, the missing 1% per year should be able to be found by 2030 – but with little leeway, and with the growing complication of struggling with issues as intangible as increasing (albeit unpriced) environmental costs of key resources and as difficult as the establishment of property rights in these resources, including plant and animal genetic resources.

Table 1.5
Indicative components of potential annual land productivity growth for major cereals (%) to the year 2030

Crop	Varietal	Irrigation[a]	Fertiliser, Management, etc[b]	Total
Rice	0.7	0.1	0.9	1.7
Wheat	0.6	0.2	1.1	1.9
Maize	1.0	0.5	0.5	2.0

a   This component has already been aggregatively 'accounted for' in the above discussion of the water resource, and is included here only to indicate the crop-specific nature of its contribution.
b   Fertiliser and its management (often, but not always, more, with better placement, timing, etc), crop management generally, including integrated pest management.

Source: Based on speculations assembled by Crosson & Anderson (1992, pp 91-99).

Lest this 'sanguine finding' seems too easy and perhaps just too convenient, let me re-emphasise some of the conditions that underlie the projections of productivity growth potential reported in Table 1.5. The varietal gains are to come from crop-improvement efforts, aided in novel ways by techniques from modern molecular biology and, at least in the case of maize, a strong involvement of private research organisations that will, in turn, depend on effective protection of the intellectual properties they will produce. There will also need to be an important contribution of private research in some of the fertiliser and management productivity gains, as well as a continuing public contribution from international and (mainly) national research agencies, for what will be increasingly knowledge-intensive input use. Needless to say, farmers will only employ such more-productive inputs to the extent that they are perceived to be profitable and not too risky, which leads us to commodity markets and trade regimes, and their uncertainties over future decades – topics for another occasion.

CONCLUSION
To seek a global perspective on world food and agriculture is thus to step back sufficiently far to look at key resource provisioning in a somewhat detached way – a step that leads one to broad-brush generalities that may not sit comfortably with a steady-as-she-goes philosophy. Those who derive their livelihood from alarmist overstatements of the urgency of many agricultural sub-system

interventions may also not wish to agree with this perspective. Realism, as I perceive it, takes one down a rather narrow path where, to stray from the resource commitments that to me seem obligatory, is to risk negative consequences for supply that are hardly conscionable. Our duty – I now conveniently lapse to the European Union as 'our,' but it clearly goes well beyond the present European Union (EU) – is to assist effectively, quickly and in some cases rather urgently, and above all magnanimously (if not altogether altruistically, because the future of Humanity is, after all, at stake). So much better to have to worry about dealing with surplus food stocks than to have to manage scarce supplies among the unfulfilled needy and hungry.

All this leads me to the general topic of 'aid' or, in official parlance, 'official development assistance.' I realise that this is not the focal theme of today's meeting but I hold strongly the view that aid cannot be allowed to slip from the agenda of a conference such as this. European assistance to agricultural development has been 'long and strong' and, it is my fervent Churchillian hope, there must be no 'withdrawal.' One cannot afford to be relaxed about such important matters, especially with so many alternative imperatives beckoning so eagerly. The 'environment' is one of these but, with a few important exceptions, it is mostly compatible with the fostering of greater agricultural productivity. 'Poverty alleviation' is another that is directly attended not only by bolstered agricultural productivity (to the extent that the poor are rural) but also by the consequently reduced prices of food staples for all.

Africa must receive a special mention, however, whether one reads Tiffen & Mortimore (1994) or Kaplan (1994). Many factors contribute to the current problems but one that will assume greater significance is an enlarged shortfall in food supply in sub-Saharan Africa. The global perspective taken thus far does not address the key question of regional distribution. In spite of the relative abundance of potential agricultural land (Table 1.3), sub-Saharan Africa will continue to lag behind other regions in per person food availabilities. Trade and aid will fill important gaps, but African food and fibre production must be boosted through investment in physical and social infrastructure, including most especially institutions, such as National Agricultural Research Systems, that efficiently provide the technology that will generate much of the needed growth in agricultural productivity.

Aid aside, what does all this prognostication mean for agricultural policy in the European Union in the post-1993 GATT era? The need for consistently growing global agricultural production is clear enough, even if the translation of this need into effective demand depends on a vast set of factors, including general economic growth and a strengthening of property rights. The scenario I have sketched suggests that we are going to 'make' it: through socially acceptable conversion of land to cropping, and some additional and refurbished irrigation; judicious but sustained investment in new agricultural knowledge to boost productivity; and an open trading regime that indeed makes a global perspective relevant.

The overview implies increasing resource scarcities and environmental challenges, particularly in heavily populated regions, expanded trade to meet local deficits and more extensively exploited national comparative advantage and, it is hoped, rather more liberalised trading systems. Any increase in protectionism will essentially diminish the global supplies of key resources. Europe, whatever its geographical range by 2030, will be a major agricultural trader, and a growing number of countries will be relying on its food exports, not to mention its industrial output that will be imported by many countries, more- and less-developed, as key agricultural inputs that will drive much of the speculated advances in productivity. How Europe manages its role in the global challenge, (it is not my field but I have read a little Atkin (1993)) as well as wrestles with its own agricultural and environmental responsibilities (Pearce, 1994), will be of great consequence and for me fascinating to observe – which is one of the reasons I am so delighted to be here today to witness part of the process in process.

REFERENCES
Atkin, M (1993) *Snouts in the trough: European farmers, the Common Agricultural Policy and the public purse,* Cambridge: Woodhead.
Bender, W H (1994) An end use analysis of global food requirements, *Food Policy* **19**(4), 381-395.
Brown, R & Kane, H (1994) *Full house: reassessing the earth's population carrying capacity.* Worldwatch Environmental Alert Series. New York: Norton.
Byerlee, D (1994) *Modern varieties, productivity, and sustainability: recent experience and emerging challenges.* Mexico 6 DF: CIMMYT
Crosson, P (1994) Future supplies of land and water for world agriculture. In: Nurul Islam (Ed) *2020 Vision.* Washington: IFPRI. (In Press).
Crosson, P & Anderson, J R (1992) *Resources and global food prospects: supply and demand for cereals to 2030.* World Bank Technical Report No. 184. Washington: World Bank.
Crosson, P & Anderson, J R (1994) Demand and supply: trends in global agriculture. *Food Policy* **19**(2), 105-119.
Downing, T E & Parry, M L (1994) Introduction: climate change and world food security. *Food Policy* **19**(2), 99-104.
FAO (1994) *Agriculture towards 2010.* Rome: FAO. (Revised draft).

Farah, J (1994) *Pesticide policies in developing countries: do they encourage excessive use?* World Bank Discussion Paper Number 238. Washington: World Bank.

Feder, G & Keck, A (In Press) Increasing competition for land and water resources: a global perspective. In: Pingate P (Ed) IRRI Conference Proceedings on *Social Science Methods in Agricultural Systems: Coping with Resource Competition in Asia.* Chiang Mai, Thailand, November 1994. Los Banōs, Phillipines: IRRI.

Francis, C A (1990) The economics of sustainable low-input farming systems. In: Francis, C A, Flora C B, & King, L D (Eds) *Sustainable agriculture in temperate zones.* New York: Wiley.

Kaplan, R D (1994) The coming anarchy. *Atlantic Monthly* **273**(2), 44-76.

Kirmani, S & Rangeley, R (1994) *International inland waters: concepts for a more active World Bank role.* World Bank Technical Paper Number 239. Washington: World Bank.

McCalla, A F (1994) *Agriculture and food needs to 2025: why we should be concerned.* Sir John Crawford Memorial Lecture, Consultative Group on International Agricultural Research, Washington, DC.

Mitchell, D O & Ingco, M D (1994) *Waiting for Malthus: the world food outlook.* Boulder, Colorado: Westview. (In Press).

Norse, D (1994) Multiple threats to regional food production: environment, economy, population? *Food Policy* **19**(2), 133-148.

Pearce, F (1994) Greening the heart of England. *New Scientist* **143** (1944), 30-35.

Tiffen, M & Mortimore, M (1994) Malthus controverted: the role of capital and technology in growth and environment recovery in Kenya. *World Development* **27**(7), 997-1010.

Umali, D L (1993) *Irrigation-induced salinity: a growing problem for development and the environment.* World Bank Technical Paper Number 215. Washington: World Bank.

United Nations (1993) *World population prospects: the 1992 revision.* New York: United Nations.

World Bank (1993) *Water resources management.* Washington: World Bank.

World Bank/UNDP (1990) *Irrigation and drainage research: a proposal.* Washington: Agriculture and Rural Development Department, World Bank.

Yudelman, M (1994) Demand and supply of foodstuffs up to 2050 with special reference to irrigation. *IIMI Review* **8**(1), 4-14.

Marshall BJ & Miller FA (Eds)(1995) *Priorities for a new century -*
agriculture, food and rural policies in the European Union. CAS Paper 31.
Reading: Centre for Agricultural Strategy.

2 The Common Agricultural Policy: the medium-term outlook in the context of future trends in international trade in agriculture

Rene Steichen

INTRODUCTION

It has given me great pleasure to accept the invitation to participate in this conference, in which we will be looking together at the priorities that will influence, indeed determine, the agricultural policy of the European Union (EU) between now and the year 2000. An ambitious and difficult undertaking, certainly, but a very pertinent one. Unless the decision-makers in politics and economics try to anticipate what the future international environment of agriculture will be, we risk being confined to short-term management instead of developing coherent policies to cope with the major changes now emerging.

When I took over as Commissioner for agriculture in January 1993, the world of European agriculture was going through an understandable period of disarray. The reform of the Common Agricultural Policy (CAP) had become inevitable because of the difficulty of controlling surpluses and budget spending under the old system, but the farming community felt that its living and working conditions were under threat. The closing stages of the Uruguay Round at the end of 1993 reinforced this mood. All that seems long ago already. You will agree with me, though, that success was very much in the balance. Would the reform start to bite, would it revive languishing markets in some products and end the continuing slide in farm incomes? It was a matter of regaining the confidence of farmers by proving in practice that what the Commission promised in launching the reform would actually happen, without breaching our international obligations. The spectre of butter mountains and wine lakes building up in Community stores, eating up the Union's budget and weighing heavily on internal and external markets, is now a thing of the past. Farmers are beginning to reap the benefits of the reform and the fruits of their efforts on the basis of a healthier balance between supply and demand.

That is a thumbnail sketch of the present picture. It is on this more solid foundation that European agriculture will be developing in the years to come. I should now like to turn to outlining the possible way forward in the medium-term. This means considering two essential parameters:

- First of all, there is the agreement reached at the end of the Uruguay Round which now has to be put into effect. This agreement will usher Community agriculture into a new era of competition with the rest of the world, while at the same time opening up new opportunities in international trade in agriculture.
- The second factor influencing the future of Community agriculture is the prospect, in the medium-term, of countries in central and eastern Europe joining the Union. The important place that agriculture and the food industry occupy in these countries and their potential for development will be a central element in preparing for and negotiating these countries' accession.

The likely impact of these two parameters will be the structure around which my talk is built.

THE NEW PROSPECTS CREATED BY THE URUGUAY ROUND

We all remember the difficult circumstances in which a compromise was finally found to complete the Uruguay Round, as signed in Marrakesh in April this year. It is now clear that, without the reform of the CAP, it would have been impossible for the EU to subscribe to the new constraints which the Uruguay Round imposes. The final overall result, seen in the light of the necessary concessions on all sides, is a satisfactory one from which our agriculture can benefit.

What, concretely, did we agree to in the Uruguay Round? One of the major issues in the trade talks was the machinery of external protection under the CAP; another was market access. On the side of current access, the idea is to allow present trade flows to continue. By contrast, minimum access is introduced for products subject to tarification. The rule will be brought in gradually, with minimum access starting at 3% of domestic consumption and finally reaching 5% when the agreement is applied in full, that is after six years. The new tarification scheme will open up the Community market more, with a reduction of customs duties by 36%, although Community preference will still be maintained at a significant level. The Union's negotiators managed to safeguard this as one of the basic principles of the CAP. The transformation of various forms of protection into customs duties will bring more transparency which will be to the advantage of all economic actors.

On internal support, the Union has undertaken to cut its overall level by 20% over six years, which is consistent with the choices made as part of the CAP reform. It ought to be remembered, however, that originally the United States (US) wanted all internal support to be abolished. The fact that the Union can continue to pay direct aid to producers as provided for in the CAP reform, as well as pursuing its present policies on rural development and structural improvement, should be seen as one of the major achievements in the Uruguay Round.

The GATT agreement also covers a further key aspect of the CAP, which is export subsidies. The Union has committed itself to cutting export subsidies by 36% over six years and to reducing the present level of subsidised exports by 21% over the same period. Despite these new constraints, which will also apply to the subsidised exports of the US, the competitiveness and quality of European products should mean that, overall, they will maintain their share of exports to the world market.

Before the Council of Ministers agreed to the GATT compromise, the question was raised as to whether our farmers might suffer further constraints as a result of new international disciplines over and above what was agreed to in the CAP reform. The Commission had already replied 'no' to this question in December 1992. The Council itself, in March 1993, agreed with the Commission's view that accepting the draft final act as amended by the Blair House accord would not involve additional sacrifices beyond those contained in the CAP reform, subject to the verification of various assumptions. The eventual agreement reached in Brussels in December 1993 clearly accorded with the Commission's position.

If we look again at the various assumptions on which the Commission based its view that our international commitments would be compatible with the CAP reform, we can see that these assumptions are beginning to be borne out by the initial results from implementing the reform. What is the situation now in the main areas of agriculture? In the cereals sector, the assumption underlying the reform was that it would bring about a marked drop in production and that more of the internal market would be supplied from domestic sources once again. As it has turned out, cereals production in 1993 and 1994 will have been under 165 million tonnes, over a million tonnes less than forecast when the reform was adopted. Compare this figure with the 180 million tonnes of the 1991 harvest. The area sown to cereals is now 32.7

million hectares, in line with the assumptions on which the reform was based. The added amount of Community grain incorporated into animal feed is estimated at 6 million tonnes for the 1993/94 marketing year. This trend should continue or even accelerate in the next few years with more consumption of pigmeat and poultrymeat. As for Community imports of cereals, these are likely to stabilise at around 4 million tonnes. Finally, some analysts had expressed fears about yields. They claimed that there was likely to be a desperate race to increase yields which would wipe out the gains from the Set-aside scheme contained in the reform package and lead to increased production. These fears have not been borne out in the first two years of the reform. The Commission believes that a continuation of the price cuts as foreseen under CAP reform (7.7% this year and a similar cut next year), and a certain degree of decoupling of premiums from production, should counter any tendency farmers may have to try to increase yields and output. In this context, it is worth noting that recent industry data show that the use of fertilisers and pesticides was very considerably down last year.

What conclusions can we draw from these trends in terms of the commitments made under GATT? As far as export discipline is concerned, only the reduction in the volume of cereals subsidised will be a potential constraint. The exports to be allowed by the end of the six years amount to 25.9 million tonnes. This figure includes the current level of food aid, at 2.5 million tonnes. However, this food aid could be increased if the need arose in the developing countries or the countries of the former Soviet Union since it is not covered by the new GATT disciplines in agriculture. Projecting Community cereals production up to the end of the agreed period, ie 1999, and even assuming annual growth of 1% in yields, the exportable surplus comes very close to the figure set under GATT.

The Commission's forecasts suggest that the Community will have to continue providing subsidies unless world prices go up significantly. If this happens, of course, it will no longer be necessary to pay out export refunds on cereals and the quantity restrictions will no longer have to be applied.

In the beef sector, intervention stocks fell by 1.1 million tonnes in early 1993 to a present level of 160 000 tonnes, and market prices have stayed firm. Despite these positive factors, an increase in production cannot be ruled out in view of the relatively favourable prices for producers. In recent years, Community imports have been around 450000 tonnes on average and exports about 1.2 million tonnes. Some of these exports have been due to the run-down of stocks over the last fourteen months, of course. Now that stocks have almost disappeared, the amounts available for export will in future be very low. By about the year 2000, imports are forecast to rise to 500 000 tonnes, while subsidised exports should drop to 817 000 tonnes in line with our GATT commitments. Save for unforeseeable events, we expect the Union to be able to meet this undertaking.

In the poultry and pigmeat sector, the fall in prices is likely to bring about an increase in demand and output. In order to fulfil the Community's GATT commitments, it will be necessary to increase the proportion of non-subsidised exports in the overall total. This should not occasion major difficulties as long as cereals prices decline further at the beginning of the 1995/96 marketing year.

The milk sector is in structural surplus and output can only be marketed by subsidising sales on both the internal and external markets. The GATT agreement will therefore have an inevitable impact on subsidised exports. At the same time, if we take milk products individually, our international commitments should not cause problems. Projected exports of butter will remain well below the ceiling set under GATT, and the same is true for skimmed-milk powder. As for cheese, the cuts in subsidised exports may indeed prove problematic. All the same, the foreseeable expansion of internal demand should cushion the impact of GATT constraints. In this connection, the cuts in quotas which were included in the reform package but have not yet been implemented should be sufficient.

Turning finally to the sectors in which reforms have not yet been introduced, the Commission has already tabled proposals for wine and fruit and vegetables which take account of the expected impact of the GATT accords. In the wine sector, the aim is to encourage production of quality wines, exports of which are likely to expand. The danger of our markets being taken away from us by wines of inferior quality sold at very low prices by non-Community countries seems relatively academic given overall consumption trends in Europe. I would also like to make a few remarks about the fresh fruit-and-vegetable sector which on the face of it, is one of the most sensitive and most directly affected because of growing competition from outside the Community. The cuts in subsidised exports and internal support should not be a very major constraint on fruit and vegetables. Only a few products are subsidised on export: tomatoes, peaches, apples, walnuts and one or two others. The impact of reduced internal support should not be significant either, given the implementing measures that have been taken. Looked at from the point of view of Community growers, and although we have to distinguish fruit and vegetables protected only by *ad valorem* customs duties and those for which there are minimum entry prices, the danger of depressed market prices only looms for a very small number of products and then only during certain periods of the year.

One can conclude then, in the light of the initial results of the reform, that the Community will be able to meet new commitments under GATT without having to impose further constraints on farmers. In the end, the Community has been able to negotiate its way to a successful conclusion of the multilateral talks without sidelining itself in terms of the international rules of the game, by having the far-sightedness and political courage to tackle a major reform process beforehand, for reasons that were mainly internal.

With the outcome of the GATT negotiations, the Community has been able to attain two fundamental goals:

- it has contributed towards constructing an international trading regime which is more market-orientated, without giving up Community preference;
- it has ensured that its international commitments are compatible with the CAP reform, retaining sufficient flexibility to be able to manage by itself the schemes which are at the base of the reformed CAP, such as direct aids and rural development.

In addition, Community exports can gradually develop their full trade potential; here I mean non-subsidised exports, where the expected rise in world prices and decline in Community price levels should increase our comparative advantage. The introduction of generalised tarification together with the provisions covering minimum access and current access should lead to a marked growth in agricultural trade worldwide. New opportunities, especially for food-industry and milk products, will be available on the US market. New markets will also open up in Japan and South Korea as a result of more transparency in the milk-product and pigmeat sectors and, because of tariff cuts, in wine and crop products. The 'double-zero' option for various spirit drinks will also benefit European businesses.

Finally, the provisions on due restraint will mean that the Community and its producers are not repeatedly faced with GATT panels and arbitration procedures. For the first time in its history, in a GATT context, the mechanisms of the CAP will be recognised as being compatible with the Community's multilateral commitments. The EU firmly intends to abide by its new international commitments against the background of the reformed CAP, and the Commission has already proposed to the Council the legislation necessary for applying the agricultural measures agreed to in the Uruguay Round. The agreements which have been negotiated are complex and therefore call for major changes to the trading arrangements contained in most of the Community market organisations. The aim of the Commission's proposals is to comply scrupulously with our obligations while at the same time preserving a high degree of flexibility in practice so as to defend our farmers' interests.

RELATIONS BETWEEN THE EU AND THE COUNTRIES OF EASTERN AND CENTRAL EUROPE IN THE AGRICULTURAL SECTOR

I would now like to turn to another international topic which is destined to assume great importance for the EU in future, and that is the question of relations with the countries of central and eastern Europe (CEE) with a view to their eventual accession. The European Council meeting in June 1993 in Copenhagen offered them the prospect of becoming members of the Union as soon as they were able to meet the obligations imposed by membership. In July 1994 the Commission sent the Council a communication and working documents on the preparation of central and eastern European countries for accession to the EU. This was a first response to the request to the Commission by the European Council in Corfu to come up with concrete proposals for implementing, in the various sectors, the Europe Agreements and the decisions taken by the European Council in Copenhagen.

As regards agriculture, the Commission had indicated that it would think specifically about future options for preparing the accession of the associate countries. I will come back to this later. Nobody will disagree that agriculture will be an extremely sensitive topic in the future accession negotiations, perhaps the most sensitive. The first reason for this is that agriculture plays an important part in these countries' economies, both in terms of GDP (Gross Domestic Product) and employment. The agricultural restructuring now in progress will be fraught with difficulties for them both politically and socially. There could be a temptation to justify it on the sole grounds of the accession requirements, although all the experts agree that such restructuring is the only way for farming in these countries to become economically viable again, regardless of whether or not they join the Union.

The second reason resides in the fears which the opening up of the CAP to the rest of Europe inspires in our own farmers. They would certainly like to receive guarantees that this opening up will not lead to fundamental changes in the mechanisms of the CAP or to a sudden flood of agricultural products onto the Community market. Independently of the agricultural crises which the CEE countries are experiencing, their potential in this sector is enormous and their products are competitive with ours and could easily destabilise our markets. It must not be forgotten that our farmers have had, in a very short space of time, to accept the changes resulting from the reform of the CAP and the commitments entered into as part of the Uruguay Round.

Before looking at how the EU could help these countries to build up their farming industries again with a view to accession I would like to comment briefly on their agricultural situation, since any proposed solution must be based on the best possible assessment of the reasons for the severe crisis in the sector. Although the OECD (Organisation for

Economic Co-operation and Development) has recently pointed to some signs of a slight upturn in agricultural production, it is highly premature to assume that the end of the crisis is in sight. While the gravity of the situation varies depending on the country and the sector under consideration, production of the main basic products has fallen sharply since the early 1990s as a result of the combined effect of the drop in domestic demand and the rise in input prices. In addition, traditional outlets in the former Soviet Union have been severely curtailed and trade between the countries themselves has also fallen off. This decline is the result of the radical changes brought about by land reform, privatisation, decentralisation and the abolition of subsidies. Restructuring and modernisation are still in progress in the farm sector and have sometimes run into serious difficulties. Despite major efforts on the part of the governments concerned, a lot still remains to be done to improve storage, processing, distribution and marketing, particularly in the case of food products. Mainly because of this generally disorganised situation, exports of agricultural produce to the EU have plummeted in recent years, while exports from the EU have increased sharply.

The CEE countries sometimes tend to lay the blame for the current difficulties their farming industry is experiencing on the CAP's alleged protectionism and its subsidy mechanisms. I believe that such a view is mistaken in the light of the real impact of our export refunds and considerably underestimates the scale of the internal difficulties encountered by their producers in making the transition from the old to the new system. It also leaves out of account the preference shown by eastern European consumers for certain western products. This does not mean, however, that in certain cases we have not been partly to blame. On the EU side, there have been complaints about the massive exports of soft fruit at dumping prices, for example, which are hitting our producers hard. Setting aside disputes of this kind, I believe that if we wish to go ahead together, the EU and the countries of eastern and central Europe will have to initiate true cooperation in an open and realistic spirit. This is necessary if we are to dedramatise the agricultural aspects of the future accession negotiations and prevent the continued deterioration of their production systems and trade deficits from jeopardising the progress of economic and political reform in the countries of eastern and central Europe.

What form might such cooperation take? I think it is important to distinguish, as the Commission in fact has done, between long-term and short-term measures.

Turning first to the long term, the Commission stated in July this year that it was necessary to examine very carefully the ways it could propose of facilitating agricultural convergence so as to prepare these countries for accession, in view of the possible implications of the various options both for the development of the CAP and for the agricultural policies of the associate countries. In my view this process must be a long-term one and be based on the principle of acceptance by them of the *acquis communautaire*, that is to say the principles on which the CAP is based. The Commission staff are at present examining these matters in order to prepare a detailed communication which the Commission will submit next year. Without committing the Commission at this stage, I feel there are two major complementary approaches to be explored:

- a system based simply on the free play of market forces advocated by some is, in my view, economically and politically unrealistic. In fact, with the exception of New Zealand, there is no industrialised country today which manages without some direct or indirect price support mechanisms. Even under the reformed CAP there are still certain intervention mechanisms;
- in the CEE countries, without some stabilisation of farm prices it will be difficult to create an environment in which farmers can make long-term forecasts and be encouraged to invest and produce for the market.

Consequently, a support mechanism for certain basic products should no doubt be envisaged, taking care to calculate judiciously the level of support so as not to undermine market forces. At the same time, the interdependence of internal support and trade must be taken into account, and thought must be given to the financial resources needed.

With regard to credit, it would be very useful to explore the possibility of reforming the credit system in central and eastern European countries in order to help farm enterprises out of their present financial difficulties. Without credit it will be difficult or even impossible to modernise the productive base and improve international competitiveness. A form of agricultural bank would help to resolve not only the question of inadequate cash flow but also the lack of a genuine land market. The EU could contribute advice, guidance and assistance with the establishment of agricultural land banks.

Lastly, as the EU alone will never be capable of absorbing all the exports of its eastern neighbours, ways and means, incuding financial ones, must be found for developing new trade links among those countries themselves and for restoring traditional export flows to the newly independent states of the former Soviet Union. According to the latest statistics, some CEE countries have succeeded since the second half of 1993 in restoring some of their exports to the former USSR, although at levels still far below those attained before the dissolution of Comecon.

Turning to the short-term options, you may know that as promised last July, the Commission yesterday adopted a communication to the

Council requesting a negotiating brief to adapt the agricultural trade aspects of the Europe and Interim Agreements with the CEE countries. The Commission is well aware that, if nothing is done to increase exports from these countries, political tension may get rapidly worse and jeopardise the chances of a constructive dialogue for agricultural cooperation in the long term. Such tension was generated in the past when the Community introduced animal health protection measures, which were seen by the associated countries as trade protectionism. In this connection the Commission is currently preparing framework agreements with the associated countries in order to establish a basis for equivalence and cooperation which should greatly facilitate exports of crop and livestock products from the CEE countries to the countries of the Union in the future. Most of the framework agreements could be submitted for adoption by the Council before the end of the year.

Coming back to the negotiating brief for the adaptation of the agricultural sections of the Europe Agreements, it is essential to take account of the following points:

- the Europe Agreements must be adjusted to the new situation created by the conclusion of the Uruguay Round. The forthcoming implementation of the latter Agreement will create an international environment more favourable to agricultural trade, and this will benefit the central and eastern European economies. In the context of cooperation between the Union and central and eastern Europe, it will be necessary to evaluate the repercussions of the concessions accepted during the Uruguay Round on the reciprocal preferences granted in the Europe Agreements;

- in addition, the Europe Agreements must be adjusted to the enlarged Union. Specifically, the arrangements concluded by the future Member States in the context of bilateral preferential agreements with the CEE countries must be integrated into the main Agreements;

- the Commission will also look closely, with the CEE countries concerned, at the reasons why the tariff quotas opened by the Union have not been fully taken up and how this situation can be rapidly improved. Finally, it will also examine, with the authorities, the reasons behind the significant growth of agricultural exports from the Union to the CEE countries. It will then be necessary to reach agreement with the CEE countries on mechanisms whereby specific cases of severe imbalance in agricultural trade flows can be remedied;

- finally, the Commission proposes instituting an early-warning mechanism for soft fruit, in order to reduce the risk of sudden disruption or interruption of exports. In order for such a mechanism to be effective, encouragement should be given to the creation of associations of exporters in the CEE countries. They

43

would then be able to organise themselves more effectively and take the necessary measures more promptly.

I think this shows that the Commission has already taken certain initiatives for the short term to prepare a strategy for the progressive convergence of the farming sectors of the Union and the associated countries. Contacts and exchanges of ideas must be stepped up not only between the public authorities but also between representatives of the farming sectors in general. I have, myself, visited the ministries of agriculture of the Visegrad countries and Baltic states to promote the idea of agricultural cooperation. I have always encountered keen interest in such initiatives.

We are preparing for a long-term task with many obstacles. Other initiatives will be proposed by the Commission, in particular on the options for long-term cooperation. The prospective debate will no doubt be a lively one. The farmers in the Union must appreciate that it is preferable to have more highly organised competitors in the east with a livelihood and purchasing power rather than no competitors at all and possibly no markets either. For the central and eastern European farmers it would be dangerous to imagine that the EU alone can ensure the recovery of their farming industries, as if the causes of the crisis were essentially external. It would be equally unrealistic to think that the EU alone can absorb all the agricultural goods produced in the associated countries. Despite the criticisms levelled against the CAP by producers in the east, I must stress that it is in the long-term interest of the countries of central and eastern Europe themselves for the principles and mechanisms of the CAP to be maintained. This does not mean that the CAP must not undergo some adjustments where necessary to facilitate accession. Any analysis in this connection must obviously take account of the rules of international trade which may be adopted after the period of implementation of the Uruguay Round agreement.

CONCLUSION

After this review of the two major issues that will influence the development of the CAP over the coming years, I would like to add a few remarks about the trend of world agricultural trade. I have already referred to the importance of the agricultural potential of the CEE countries. The scope for progressive and non-conflictual growth of agricultural trade between the CEE countries and the countries of the EU will also depend on the ability of the CEE countries to revive traditional trade flows with each other and with the countries of the former USSR.

More generally, the Uruguay Round is expected to have a positive impact on world trade. Analyses show that world demand for food and agrifood products should double in the next ten years. Taking account of population growth and economic expansion in south-east Asia, the FAO forecasts a significant rise in demand for cereals. This will inevitably affect world trade flows, in that south-east Asia, above all China, South Korea, India and Indonesia, will probably be unable to meet its own requirements. But, of course, we do not yet know what impact technical progress and genetic improvement will have on yields of, for instance, rice in those regions. Furthermore, the choices of south-east Asian governments as regards the types of crop to develop - cereals, maize, or rice? - will undoubtedly affect international markets.

The EU at present exports 10% of its agricultural production, and 18% if agrifood products are included. I am convinced that, in the context of expanding world demand, our exporters will be able to find new outlets for our products, whether basic commodities or processed food products. New needs will also continue to emerge on markets where Community products are very competitive, such as dairy products or biscuits, for which we hold 60% of the world market. I think the new rules on international trade will stimulate competition and the search for new outlets by businesses in the EU and agricultural exports should therefore expand in the medium term.

DISCUSSION

Sir John Quicke (Farmer and CAS Advisory Committee) referred to Mr Steichen's comment that CEE countries felt it was in their interest for the CAP to continue. He saw some difficulties in this and invited the Commissioner to explain further.

M Steichen said that he was reflecting discussions with Ministers representing most of the CEE countries, who had expressed concern about their crop price and marketing arrangements that provide greater benefits for speculators than for producers. They had therefore expressed interest in suitable support mechanisms for their basic products, a form of aid for restructuring of farms, and credit facilities for land transactions. Discussions with these countries continue.

Ms Annabel Holt (Annabel's Crusade for the Environment) proposed to Mr Steichen that the European Commission should seek a six-year moratorium against challenge to animal and environmental issues, consistent with the moratorium against challenge to agriculture included in the GATT Uruguay Round.

M Steichen in reply felt that this matter is not linked with GATT, and referred to the historical differences of approach on animal welfare matters between the northern and southern countries in the EU. He expressed optimism about the outcome of current discussions based on veterinary advice, which tended to place greater importance on the conditions under which animals are transported than on the duration of transportation. He recognised, however, that the UK continued to stress the importance of time limitation and confirmed that this factor is being taken into account in the ongoing discussions.

Mr Peter Brown (Agricultural business consultant), who had recently participated in a trade mission to Russia said that he returned with a strong impression that the overwhelming need is for inward supplies of food rather than the development of food exports. He accordingly asked the Commissioner to comment on the prospects of aid in relation to feeding the population, and the likely time scale for the entry of Russia into international commodity trading.

M Steichen in reply outlined the EC long-standing policy of providing food aid in cases of real and immediate need, with a preference for co-operation in various ways to assist with the development of self-supporting agricultural production, processing and marketing systems. He felt unable to make a specific forecast for Russia but expressed the view that the development of normally functioning agricultural sectors in the CEE countries is likely to take at least fifteen years.

Mrs Pippa Woods (Small Farmers' Association) said that it is generally assumed that further reforms of the CAP, possibly in 1996, seem likely to reduce farming support because of the public perception that there is no logical reason for encouraging food production when (at least in the short-term) there is over-production on world markets. She expressed concern that there is little sympathy for the social aspects of farmers in producing from their land and caring for the countryside, and asked Mr Steichen for his view about the future of support for farmers.

M Steichen commented that following unsuccessful efforts during the 1980s to reduce the support of the agricultural sector, Finance Ministers decided in 1988 on an 'agricultural guideline' which prescribed that the agricultural budget must not increase by more than 74% of the rise in total budget, ie an increase of 3% in total budget limits the increase of the agricultural budget to 2.2%. He felt that this policy, which ensures a fair return for farmers in relation to other industrial and social categories, should be maintained. He also considered that, contrary to earlier fears, the 1992 CAP reforms are working well, farmers on average are content with the outcome, and accordingly he sees no justification for further reforms.

Marshall BJ & Miller FA (Eds)(1995) *Priorities for a new century - agriculture, food and rural policies in the European Union.* CAS Paper 31. Reading: Centre for Agricultural Strategy.

3 Environmental and agricultural policies

Martin Holdgate

INTRODUCTION: A MATTER OF DEFINITION

I have been asked to talk about environmental and agricultural policies. The presumption is that they are somehow different. Is this so? How? Why? Albert Einstein is said to have commented that 'environment is everything that isn't me'. The environment is the whole encircling world - the world of nature, driven by the sun's energy, within which we and all other life forms live, and the built world, created by human ingenuity over the millennia. We are all part of one another's environment.

But when we speak of 'environmental policies' today, we usually mean one of three things:

- measures to protect people, crops, livestock, wildlife and natural ecosystems against damage from pollution, or from the knock-on effects of pollution, like ultraviolet-B radiation pouring through a weakened ozone screen or climate change caused by greenhouse gas accumulation;
- measures to maintain natural beauty, the diversity of wild nature (described by today's new buzz-term 'biodiversity'), and the historic features of town and country;
- measures to curb urban and industrial developments, and especially urban and motorway sprawl.

When we speak of 'agricultural policies' we normally mean measures to maintain the productivity – both biological and financial – of agriculture.

A LITTLE HISTORY

Agriculture takes place within the environment. Over the thousands of years of human history it has been the foundation of the process we call development - the changing by human skill of aspects of the natural world so that it is better able to support human life. Development is a process of increasing the carrying capacity of the environment for people. Agriculture has been central to development. Think simply of cereal yields. Under the old open-field system in around 1200 AD, our ancestors maybe gathered in 0.5 tonnes per hectare of wheat (Cooke, 1970). With the new seed drills and four-course rotation of the 18th Century, the output rose to around 1.75 tonnes per hectare. With fertilisers and selective weed killers and new short-straw varieties, the production lifted to around 3 tonnes per hectare in the 1950s. In 1990 it had reached between 6.5 and 7.5 tonnes per hectare in Germany, France, the UK and the Netherlands (Prescott, 1994).

This process has been a liberator of humanity from all the ills and uncertainties of insecure food supplies. It has allowed much higher population densities to live sustainably. Some thirty years ago the distinguished American ecologist, HT Odum, compared the capacity of four environmental systems to support people. The systems were a tropical rain forest, Ugandan grasslands, Indian monsoon croplands and United States intensive agriculture. The population supported? From a few hunter-gatherers per square kilometre in the forest, to 25 pastoralists per square kilometre on the savannas, to 230 villagers and 30 city dwellers supported by a square kilometre of rainfed cultivation in the monsoon zone, to 60 people on the land and 2000 in the city, sustained per square kilometre in the USA (Institute of Ecology, 1971).

Of course this process of development has meant environmental change. About 46 million square kilometres of land were forested before humanity began to develop agriculture. By 1970 some 15% of that forest had gone. About 6.5 million square kilometres had been cleared in the temperate zones - notably in Europe and north America. Worldwide, some 16 million square kilometres of forest and grassland were converted from natural vegetation to farmland by 1980 (Tolba *et al*, 1992). In Britain, according to Oliver Rackham's fascinating *History of the countryside* (1986), most of the 'wildwood' was stripped from high altitudes and river valleys in Bronze Age times, and half of the English wildwood had probably gone by the early Iron Age (500 BC). By the time of the Domesday Survey, the distribution of woodland in large parts of England was probably much as it is now. Outside a few remaining areas of extensive forest like the Weald, Chilterns, Arden and the Forest of Dean the landscape was farmland with islands of wood. Of course these processes of conversion had their negative sides. There was a lot of erosion in Britain during forest clearance in

Bronze Age and later times. The soil profiles in many upland areas were truncated, and much alluvial material was transferred from hilltops to valley bottoms. We were not alone. Plato mourned the damage done by deforestation in Attica in classical Greek times, while badly managed irrigation leading to salinisation and waterlogging was probably a factor in the population crash - a drop of some 90% -in Mesopotamia between 800 and 1300 AD (Whitmore *et al*, 1990). Today, an area as big as India has been lost from productive agriculture through misuse and a tract three times the size of India yields less than it could and should (Tolba *et al*, 1992).

My point is that over most of the world and throughout most of history, agriculture has been the foundation of human development, but that it has not always used the essential resources of soil and water well. This remains the case today. And as Professor Anderson's paper demonstrates, if we are to curb the poverty that afflicts around a billion people today, and cater for a population increase from today's 5.8 billion to the projected 8.5-10 billion in the second half of the next century, we shall have to about double world food production. And we shall have to do so sustainably - without losing more Indias. This is likely to mean great increases in production from the more fertile lands suited to intensive cultivation rather than more encroachment on the land that retains natural vegetation. The problem is that there is a severe mismatch between human population distribution and growth and areas with the capacity to produce more food, and the poorer countries lack money to buy food from elsewhere. Hence, the enhancement of food production has to go hand-in-hand with economic growth and more open trading systems.

Two conclusions emerge from this opening scenario. First agricultural policy is inevitably a part of environmental policy because - *reductio ad absurdum* - you can't have agriculture without the environment and you won't spend much time talking about environmental policy unless the people are fed. Second, whatever is done in Britain and in the rest of Europe has to be seen in the context of a rapidly changing world. My thesis is, therefore, that the debate is not about agricultural policies versus environmental ones, but the place of agriculture and of particular agricultural techniques **within** environmental policy as a whole, and especially within - to use another buzz-term - 'sustainable development'. Development, to quote the World Commission on Environment and Development (1987) 'that meets the needs of the present without jeopardizing the ability of future generations to meet their own needs'.

THE CONFLICT BETWEEN AGRICULTURAL AND ENVIRONMENTAL POLICIES

It is here that conflict has arisen between the agricultural community and the champions of conservation - whether of wildlife or the landscape. It is worth reminding ourselves why. Modern agriculture has developed dramatically since the 1940s. That development has two principal roots - one socioeconomic and the other scientific. Many people here today will know far more than I do about the impact of the depression in the 1930s on the life of rural communities in this country. Many more of us have some memory of the problems of feeding the population of Britain during the 1939-1945 war. At the end of that war, there was, I believe, a social determination, expressed at a high level in Government, that we would never again neglect our agriculture and revert to pre-war dependence on foreign imports. The farm support schemes then adopted were of course very different from those now in operation under the Common Agricultural Policy (CAP) of the European Union (EU), but the goal is the same. We find it throughout Europe, not just in the Union. In Switzerland and Finland, for example, agricultural support is an important area of public policy and public expenditure. The second root is scientific. Thanks to science, the yields of crops and livestock have been boosted enormously. Some of the means are genetic - expressed in new high-yielding short-straw cereals, and strains that do not shed their grains even when over-ripe. Some are chemical - improved synthetic fertilisers and a wide spectrum of ever more selective pesticides. Some are engineered - better machinery, permitting a vastly reduced labour force to handle the vastly increased production of vastly enlarged fields.

Many of our problems stem from these gains in efficiency - for we have become an urban, or at least a non-agricultural community. In pre-industrial times, virtually everyone either lived in the countryside or had close kin that depended on agriculture. Today, under 2% of the British population work in agriculture. For most of the population the countryside is a place to visit for recreation - a landscape to look at. But the countryside is less beautiful than it was. At least, many people think so. The arable revolution has not only lost us trees, hedgerows, ponds and stone walls, but all the little patches of rough ground that used to be rich in birds and butterflies. The transformation of pastures and meadows by reseeding and copious applications of nitrogenous fertiliser has lost us the herb-rich, flower-filled meadows that I can still remember from, for example, the limestone country of what used to be Westmorland. The geographical specialisation of farming means that you can drive through a dozen parishes in eastern England and never see a cow. And the town-dweller not only sees these things but, perhaps more to the point, reads how dreadful they are in a literature - a litany - of environmental complaint. Some of the books have become famous. The first and perhaps most famous of all of all - Rachel Carson's seminal work, *Silent Spring* (1962) shocked people by its allegation that the wonder chemicals, DDT, dieldrin and their relatives, were destroying birdlife. In Britain the deaths of foxes in fox-hunting Leicestershire, from eating pigeons poisoned by persistent organochlorines, sent shock waves through the rural community and led directly to the creation of the Nature Conservancy's Pesticides and Wild Life Section under the distinguished naturalist, Dr Norman Moore. At that time the accusation that these wonder chemicals could be 'Bad Things' was angrily rejected by the agrochemical industry. We now know that while pesticides bring immense benefits, they also need much stricter controls than was then thought necessary.

People read of other damage to be laid at agriculture's door. Stubble burning brought farming a bad press - not, incidentally, eased by the fact that now that the incorporation of straw residues into soil has been forced on a reluctant farming community, their value in enhancing soil organic content is being recognised. The contamination of aquifers with nitrogen, making water blending or treatment an expensive necessity if potable water supplies are to stay within EU health standards; the eutrophication of rivers, lakes and estuaries, leading in turn to dangerous 'red tides' in places like the Kattegat; all these feed the fires of criticism. It is intensified by press reports of financial wastefulness in the CAP - allegations, for example, that the CAP costs every citizen of the EU £250 a year, yet that the farmer is not the main beneficiary because in 1990 48% of the CAP budget went on storing surpluses and subsidising exports.

People's imaginations are fired by the new prospect of the twin peaks of Butter Mountain and Mont Boeuf, seen across Wine Lake. And they strongly dislike the notion that we are paying subsidies to farmers (and also to foresters, but they are not today's target) to destroy our nature and our landscape. It is not helped by the view that the agricultural community is - to quote a long-gone Minister - 'featherbedded'. Almost all industries are required under the 'Polluter Pays Principle' to internalise the costs of their actions - to pay the costs of meeting the standards set for emissions to the environment. Yet when nitrogenous fertilisers contaminate chalk aquifers, and then drinking water, the consumer pays - twice : on water bills for water treatment, and in general taxation for payment to farmers in Nitrate Sensitive Areas. When run-off from farmland leads to ecological changes in estuaries and coastal seas, it is the fishing community, the tourist industry and wildlife that bear the costs. People ask why the agricultural industry should not be made to internalise these costs, as other industries have been made to do.

The third area of environmental criticism is the most serious of all. It arises from the argument that intensive modern agriculture may be ecologically unsustainable in the long term because its use of chemicals - fertilisers and pesticides - is stressing soil systems beyond the limits of their resilience. It is linked to the argument that the marginal cost of subsidy to agriculture exceeds the marginal benefits and hence that we would gain net benefit by spending less, applying less chemicals, securing marginally lower yield, but having a more diverse and resilient countryside.

Quite a lot of people in this room no doubt hold as an article of faith that the beauties of the English countryside have been made by farming, are maintained by farming, and would be lost without farming. It is true that the wonderful landscapes we cherish were carved by agriculture out of the wild wood. It is true that many of our most beautiful scenes were moulded by caring landowners over the past three centuries. But is this still true? Or was Professor Bryn Green right when he wrote in 1981 that 'it is now the dominant rural uses themselves - agriculture and forestry - which present ever-growing threats to the countryside'?

The debate, or argument, is not really between environmental and agricultural policy at a fundamental level - everyone cheerfully assents to the proposition that we all want healthy agriculture in a healthy environment filled with healthy wildlife - but at the level of detail. I want now to be constructive and look at ways in which environmental and agricultural policies are coming together, and then, finally, to flash a torch on the green lane ahead.

THE RECONCILIATION OF ENVIRONMENTAL AND AGRICULTURAL POLICIES

Attempts at reconciliation are nothing new. I remember taking part in a weekend conference at Silsoe in the 1960s, masterminded by Derek Barber and Eric Carter, in which three syndicates of conservationists, farmers and agricultural advisers, walked a farm and drew up alternative management plans - for maximum agricultural return, for maximum nature conservation compatible with viable farming, and for the 'common sense' balance of both. That meeting was one spur to the creation of the Farming and Wildlife Advisory Group (FWAG) (with or without an extra initial 'F' for Forestry), which have undoubtedly done valuable work.

Where now? There have been several big strategic documents in recent years that try to plot a course for farming within the overall process of 'sustainable development'. If I may begin with one I was concerned with personally, in 1991 IUCN - The World Conservation Union, the United Nations Environment Programme and the World Wide Fund for Nature published a second World Conservation Strategy entitled *Caring for the earth. A Strategy for sustainable living*

(IUCN/UNEP/WWF, 1991). It has a simple message. We need development to ease the problems of the billion or more people who live in poverty and to cater for the 3 to 5 billion we are warned will be added to the world population during the next 50 years. But that development must provide real improvement in the quality of life and must conserve the vitality and diversity of the Earth. To quote: 'We need development that is both people-centred, concentrating on improving the human condition, and conservation based, maintaining the variety and productivity of nature. We have to stop talking about conservation and development as if they were in opposition, and recognize that they are essential parts of one indispensable process'. *Caring for the earth devotes* a chapter to how we can use the world's farmlands and rangelands sustainably. It makes fourteen points summarised briefly as:

- countries should draw up national strategies for sustainable living;
- the best farmland should be protected for agriculture, and effective soil and water conservation should be promoted through good land husbandry;
- where marginal lands are already being used by agriculture, its impact must be carefully regulated;
- the productivity and sustainability of rainfed farming should be increased;
- integrated crop and livestock farming systems, with more efficient fertiliser use, should be encouraged;
- integrated pest management should be promoted, and the use of fertilisers, pesticides and herbicides should be controlled by both regulation and market incentives;
- genetic resources must be conserved both in their natural habitats and in gene banks, botanic gardens and collections, and this action must be coordinated and supported internationally;
- support for farmers should be switched from price support to conservation support; they should be helped to care for soil, water, wild resources like fisheries, and natural beauty; and non-farm employment should be made available in rural communities.

Nothing very radical there! What about *Agenda 21*, the resounding 650-page Action Plan for the 21st Century adopted by the largest-ever gathering of Heads of State and Government in Rio de Janeiro in June 1992 (Robinson, 1994)? It also emphasises that 'the integration of environment and development concerns, and greater attention to them, will lead to the fulfilment of basic needs, improved living standards for all, better protected and managed ecosystems, and a safer and more prosperous future'. I am not sure whether that statement is in the realm of pious hope, extreme optimism or political manifesto - but at least, preamble safely passed, *Agenda 21* does get down to some prescriptions for agriculture. It calls for an integrated approach to land use. 'National Sustainability Strategies' are a means to that end. It calls for action to combat the wasteful destruction and mismanagement of forests, and to halt desertification. It has a long chapter about meeting agricultural needs without destroying the land. What actions? The list is not unlike that in *Caring for the earth*. Let me tick them off headline by headline:

- integrate sustainable development into agricultural policy and planning;
- ensure people's participation;
- improve farm productivity and diversify rural employment;
- harmonise land resources planning;
- conserve and rehabilitate land;
- conserve plant and animal genetic resources, and use them sustainably;
- use integrated pest management;
- employ sustainable plant nutrition;
- move the energy mix in rural areas from fuelwood, dung and muscle power to a blend of renewable and fossil fuels;
- evaluate the effects of ozone layer depletion (and let me add, climate change) on agriculture.

Splendid. But the problem is, of course, that these are headlines while we have to get down to real action on the real earth. What, for example, has the United Kingdom (UK) Government done about translating these prescriptions, that John Major broadly endorsed in Rio, into national plans? The answer is in the shape of a volume slim relative to *Agenda 21* but still running to 265 pages, entitled *Sustainable development: the UK strategy* (Anon, 1994a). Let me turn rapidly to page 106, where Chapter 15 on Agriculture starts. This is not to deny that there is not a great deal else that is relevant in earlier and later sections, for of course action to curb pollution, to control urban sprawl, to prevent climate change - these and many other actions are highly relevant to the land and what grows on it. I shall indeed look in a minute at climate change, and whether the green lane to the future may become a dry and dusty one. But back to our national strategy for sustainable agriculture. The most important thing about this Chapter (and the whole strategy) is that it accepts that any UK action has to be taken within the context of the EU, and indeed of the world as a whole. Sustainable agriculture in Britain depends on how the CAP is developed and applied. But the goals for sustainable agriculture are clear:

- to provide an adequate supply of good-quality food and other products in an efficient manner;
- to minimise consumption of non-renewable and other resources, including by recycling;

- to safeguard the quality of soil, water and air;
- to preserve, and where feasible enhance, biodiversity and the appearance of the landscape, including the UK's archaeological heritage.

This vision, I note, is shared by the Government and the non-governmental movement, at least in the shape of WWF-UK and BirdLife International, who produced a statement in March this year (Dixon & Murray, 1994). They called for a prosperous rural economy, which produces sufficient quantities of high quality food for the nutritional needs of Europe and contributes to an equitable trading system; an integration of land uses; a sustainable agriculture which internalises the environmental and social costs of its activities, applies the 'Polluter Pays Principle', and is subsidised only for achieving wider social and environmental objectives rather than for food production in itself; and a wildlife-rich countryside within a diverse, prosperous and peopled landscape. The Government (and I must not make the Minister's speech for him, but this is what the Strategy says) 'will encourage environmentally sensitive agriculture, and will work for further CAP reform to reduce levels of support and integrate fully environmental considerations'. To this end, we now have a broad raft of policies and special schemes in operation here:

- there are 33 Environmentally Sensitive Areas (ESAs) covering over 2.7 million hectares, where incentives are offered to farmers to farm in ways that maintain or enhance natural beauty, biological diversity and historic interest;
- payments can be made for management of Sites of Special Scientific Interest (SSSIs) to safeguard species and habitats;
- in Nitrate Sensitive Areas (NSAs), farmers are being paid to restrict their activities (I am not sure that this does not breach the 'Polluter Pays Principle');
- some 60 000 hectares are within the scope of the Countryside Stewardship Scheme to protect habitats and landscapes;
- farm woodland schemes encourage the planting of new woods;
- the Farm and Conservation Grant Scheme gives grants for pollution control equipment and environmental improvements such as hedge planting.

The Strategy also records a widening of the system, with more ESAs, more NSAs, a Moorland Scheme, a Countryside Access Scheme, a Habitat Scheme, and an Organic Aid Scheme.

These schemes, and the commitment to sustainable agriculture within a healthy environment, are of course welcome. But I have to say that sceptical noises can still be heard in the green undergrowth. They particularly concern the environmental benefits to be expected from the 1992 reform of the CAP. According to a report prepared for WWF (Baldock & Beaufoy, 1992) the Regulations underpinning the new support arrangements make little or no reference to the environment. Only Set-aside land is subject to environmental conditions and these are minimal. An opportunity has been missed for attaching environmental conditions to income payments under both the livestock and arable support regimes. It is difficult to forecast precisely how farmers will react to the new rules.

There has been a particular debate about Set-aside. As I understand it, the basic policy is that farmers producing more than 92 tonnes of arable crops (as most British arable farmers do) will only be eligible for their arable area payments if they set aside 15% of their arable land. But this 15% was, under the initial scheme, to be rotated around the farm, not returning to the same area for at least 5 years. The land must be out of 'beneficial use' for a minimum of 7 months, but cared for so as to maintain 'good cropping conditions'. Land set aside has to be managed 'to ensure protection of the environment', but what does this mean? A one-year break in cultivation will certainly not permit the return of many of the wildlife species - plant and animal - whose loss has impoverished our arable landscape. Any area of land left to nature for one year will simply grow a crop of opportunistic, widely dispersed, plants. Moreover, many farmers seem set on curbing what they see as excessive weed growth by some kind of growth-regulating herbicide. Really, what we are seeing is a reversion to the old practice of fallowing. It is unlikely to do much for plant, insect or bird diversity, although it is fair to add that in this country the Ministry of Agriculture has specified that environmental features such as hedges, trees, ponds, streams and ditches on land adjoining that set aside must be maintained. And the FWAG have suggested that some birds like larks, finches, partridges, thrushes and lapwings might benefit - depending on just how the land is used.

If we want to restore the diversity and beauty of the farmscape, something more will be needed. We shall have to consider some permanent Set-aside for new wild habitats. The Farm Woodlands Scheme could be valuable here, if it leads to planting of native broadleaved species, not simply conifers. It would do no harm to leave odd corners to nature, as what we used to call 'rough'. The aim cannot be to restore the old landscape - that would not be sensible or practicable, but we can insert new patches and corridors of wild habitat into the farmed environment, alongside the relict patches of wild habitat that persist. We must cherish these latter, for example with a firm presumption in law against the destruction of SSSIs or of landscape features of high quality. We should blend the farm support schemes under the reformed - and further to be reformed - CAP with the more narrowly conservationist measures in Europe like the Habitats Directive and the Birds Directive. They should all be complementary to one another.

Patience will be needed. Remember that many cherished, species-rich, habitats like chalk and limestone grassland are nutrient-poor. The soils that used to support them now have greatly elevated nitrogen concentrations. Their profiles have been altered by cultivation. Just stopping cultivating downland fields and leaving them to nature will not speedily restore a downland turf. It is likely to need decades of leaching, and close grazing. Similarly, abandoning a lowland field will not create a woodland in less than fifty years. Management will be needed, and that means harnessing the skills of the ecologist and the farmer. The FWAGs have an obvious role here.

None-the-less, I believe that there is now a strong desire, in Britain and elsewhere in the EU, for a new kind of environmental policy for the farmed landscape. A policy that blends prosperous farming with landscape quality, natural beauty and rich wildlife. And we have some achievements to show in Europe. For example, our continent was the creator of the kind of National Park that is essentially a protected landscape - a place where natural beauty and wildlife diversity is cherished, but in a farmed and inhabited countryside that is the basis for many trades, and for much recreation. This is also the welcome approach in the recently published Action Plan for protected Areas in Europe (IUCN, 1994). We do not have great wilderness areas like Yosemite, Yellowstone or the Serengeti, but we do have a Lake District and a Schwarzwald. For densely populated continents, ours is the better model.

One thread that runs through *Agenda 21, Caring for the earth*, and many national Strategies for Sustainability is what we might call - if our semantic stomachs are strong - 'subsidiarity' - getting the policy debate into the communities that live on, value, and manage the land; getting the national strategy turned into local action plans. The UK Biodiversity Action Plan (Anon, 1994b) emphasises the need for wide involvement of the community, and for restoring habitats in the urban and peri-urban zones, and amid the farmlands, as well as maintaining the more outstanding habitats like SSSIs. But when it comes to the precise pattern, why not let the local community discuss what they want and help them turn their consensus into action? We call this 'Primary Environmental Care' in the environment business. We stress that the plans and strategies that work best are those that the local community - farmers, landowners, village residents, hoteliers, local businesses and local conservationists - feel they **own**. Why not back the raft of support schemes with grant to local groups to get together and work out plans for sustainability and the conservation of biological diversity that fit their areas? They might surprise all of us!

The key is **integration**. Clearly, there is some way to go in the EU in developing the CAP and, among other changes, giving it an environmental heart. But the Union can set a world example by demonstrating that it is possible to have integrated policies for the rural environment, in which agriculture is productive, prosperous and sustainable, within a wider environment that is biologically diverse and beautiful. The countryside should provide food for both the body and the spirit. If we can get that right in Western Europe, we shall do good to others beyond ourselves. There is an urgent need for such a model in Eastern Europe as the economies there struggle to modernise themselves, and as their agriculture moves into a market economy. Those countries are some of the most diverse biologically in Europe, and have large areas of outstanding scenery and wildlife habitat. It would be a tragedy if they copied our mistakes just as we were beginning to move to new things.

THE WIDER CONTEXT
But what we do here in European agriculture will be immensely influenced by what happens in the wider world. And we have some major uncertainties to consider. Indeed, the idea that we have surplus land to set aside may be false - or transient. There are three reasons for this:

- first, sustainable agriculture, even in Europe, may prove to be less intensive agriculture in which we apply fewer agrochemicals, adopt semi-organic farming and integrated pest control, and accept somewhat lower yields per hectare for the sake of landscape quality and environmental health;
- or second, we may have to maximise food production in Europe because we have the kind of farmland that can be used intensively to help meet the estimated requirement for twice today's world food production half a century hence;
- or third, our productivity may be forced down, our cropping patterns altered, and our natural habitats transformed by climate change.

We need to debate the prospects for all three, but because of time I will only talk about the third, the largest uncertainty that confronts us.

What's that I hear you say? 'We thought all that speculation had been dismissed because greenhouse warming is being cut out by sulphate aerosols and more clouds?' Sorry. No. Do remember that it is the greenhouse gases in the atmosphere that make the Earth habitable for our kind of life. Thanks to the natural greenhouse effect of water vapour and carbon dioxide, the Earth is about 30°C warmer than it would otherwise be. Since pre-industrial times, human activity has greatly increased the atmospheric concentrations of carbon dioxide, nitrous oxide and methane as well as the artificial greenhouse gases, chlorofluorocarbons, in the atmosphere. We are committed to the equivalent of at least a doubling in carbon dioxide. It seems to me absurd to argue that although the natural greenhouse effect makes the planet habitable, the effective doubling of concentrations of carbon dioxide from pre-industrial levels will have no effect. The best estimates are that while the increased reflectivity of clouds and the reduction in incoming radiation by sulphate aerosols may reduce warming in the industrial belt of the northern hemisphere, they will not stop it. Globally the projection of a 1.5°C increase in mean temperature over the next 50 years is about right. Some models suggest that rainfall may increase by about 10% in many regions, but fall on fewer days, leading to more flash floods. And the seasonal differences may increase - southern England, for example, may have warmer wetter winters, and warmer drier summers, and the same holds even more so for the near continent like France, Germany, Switzerland and northern Italy.

The big issue is how such changes will affect the distribution of farming patterns, forests, and wild ecosystems. Some of the implications are disturbing. A 1.5°C rise in mean temperature spread over the next 50 years does not sound much, but this would displace the limits of tolerance of species some 225 kilometres polewards in North America and Europe, and would elevate the limits of crop cultivation by some 200 m in the UK, and a rather larger figure in the Alps (Parry, 1990). Some models suggest that if changes of rather larger magnitude were to occur, the boreal coniferous forest in Europe would be limited to the far north of Scandinavia, and to high altitudes, with the broadleaved forests displaced northwards from England into Scotland and southern Scandinavia and a mediterranean-type vegetation established in southern England.

One can only assume that the agricultural limits will shift similarly. Wheat and barley production, on that basis, would become much more competitive in the Nordic countries. Silage maize might be capable of growth almost anywhere in lowland England and Wales, or even eastern Scotland. Vineyards would do well in southern Britain. But France and Spain might be more prone to desertification. And the farming community will have to be ready for quite considerable husbandry changes.

Wild nature would be affected greatly. And the problem is not only the magnitude of the projected changes but their rate. For even these changes that don't sound very much are in fact bigger than we have evidence for in such a short period at any time in the past 20 000 years, if not longer. On average, dominant trees like the American eastern hemlock, maple or oak have only spread at a rates of around 25 km per century since the last ice age. Some trees, such as birches, may have kept up with the retreating ice, but others appear to have moved much more slowly (Bennett, 1986). Rapid greenhouse-induced climate change may well, therefore, disrupt ecosystems by reducing productivity and regeneration at the 'trailing edge', where conditions are no longer tolerable for dominant species, while leaving slowly-dispersing dominants behind the advancing margin of increased favourability. No doubt opportunistic species will do well: a warming of several degrees in the Arctic would no doubt lead to rapid spread of birch and willow species and also favour wind-dispersed plants like willow herb, but a lot of valued species would tend to be squeezed out and biological diversity would decline. A lot of nature reserves would no longer be able to support the species for which they were created.

There is another feed-back loop to land-use practices in Europe, for changes may be called for as part of the raft of measures to curb greenhouse warming. The EU is seeking the return of our carbon dioxide emissions to the 1990 level by the year 2000. This won't be enough to cure the problem, but it is a useful first step. Some people have suggested planting new forests as one means of abstracting some of this carbon dioxide. However, the contribution this process can make seems to me to be limited. It has been calculated that to counterbalance all human additions of carbon to the atmosphere to date we would need to plant an area as big as the whole of Europe, from the Atlantic to the Urals (Nilsson, 1992). Can we really find the land, in a world which now has 5.8 billion people and may have to feed and support 8.5-10 billion by the latter part of the next century? And developing countries, embarking as many are on their own industrial development, are unlikely to agree to their land being afforested simply so that developed countries can go on building coal-burning power stations.

None the less, the proposition that we might grow energy crops, such as coppiced poplars or willows, on land not required for food production and now set aside under European agricultural policies, has attractions. This is so because by substituting wood for fossil fuel, we transfer some of our energy sources from the fossil to the active carbon cycle. Recent estimates (REAG, 1992; ETSU, 1994) suggest that energy crops might become economically attractive if electricity prices rose to between 3 and 5 pence per kilowatt hour (1991 prices). Today's basic price is around 1.5 to 2 p per KWh, but this figure is artificially low because we use a lot of old power stations that are fully depreciated, and also allow externalisation of cost through pollution. ETSU has estimated that energy crops might supply a maximum of 200 terawatt hours a year of electricity in the UK - equivalent to 60% of 1992 supply - assuming, of course, that the land can be found. That figure is undoubtedly unrealistic, but the possibility of real interest in energy woodlands remains and should be considered. It seems more than possible that this new form of cropping will therefore attract some of the land now set aside. The challenge will be to make such new coppices scenically attractive and biologically diverse as well as economically efficient.

CONCLUSIONS

My thesis is that we are just about coming to terms in Europe with the need for adjustment to our agricultural policies so as to achieve sustainability under today's conditions. The ingredients of this fusion of agricultural and environmental policy are becoming clear. Essentially they involve support for a more integrated, multi-purpose approach. They demand subsidiarity. They will probably need a reversal of some over-centralised EU policies on the genetic strains of crops and trees we plant - for genetic diversity is a positive asset in a diverse continent such as ours and encouragement needs to be given to the continued growth of locally-developed strains. Indeed, subsidiarity should mean more Union and Government support for locally-based plans under which local communities would farm and forest according to local tradition.

But I am myself convinced that the test will be how well we can adapt our policies to cope with changes in world demand, world trading and economic patterns and the world environment. The world may well have twice as many people in a marginally less favourable environment a century from now. I am not aware of any game plan in the UK or the rest of Europe that really faces up to this challenge. The minimum need is to be able to adapt our economic, social and environmental policies at least as fast as the environment itself changes. On Mr Micawber's principle - if we can do that: result, happiness. If we do not: result - disaster.

REFERENCES

Anon (1994a, b). UK Government reports.

Baldock, D & Beaufoy, G (1992) *Plough on! An environmental appraisal of the reformed CAP.* Godalming: WWF UK.

Bennett, K D (1986) The rate of spread and population increase of forest trees during the postglacial. *Phil. Trans. Roy. Soc. Lond. B* **314**, 523-531.

Carson, R (1962) *Silent spring.* London: Hamilton.

Cooke, G W (1970) The carrying capacity of the land in the year 2000. In: Taylor, L R (Ed)*The optimum population for Britain. Institute of Biology Symposium* **19**. London: Institute of Biology.

Dixon, J & Murray, G (1994) *Farming for a greener Britain: farming and environment in the 21st Century.* Sandy, Beds and Godalming: Birdlife International & WWF-UK.

ETSU (1994) *An assessment of renewable energy for the UK.* London: HMSO.

Green, B H (1981) *Countryside conservation. The protection and management of amenity ecosystems:* London: George Allen and Unwin.

Institute of Ecology (1971) *Man in the living environment. Report of the Workshop on global ecological problems.* Madison, Wisconsin: University of Wisconsin.

IUCN (1994) *Parks for life. Action for protected areas in Europe.* Gland, Switzerland: IUCN - The World Conservation Union.

IUCN/UNEP/WWF (1991) *Caring for the earth: a strategy for sustainable living.* Gland, Switzerland: IUCN-The World Conservation Union.

Nilsson, A (1992) *Greenhouse earth.* Chichester: John Wiley & Sons.

Odum H T (1967) Energetics of world food production. *The world food problem* **3**, 44-95.

Parry, M (1990). *Climate change and world agriculture.* London: Earthscan.

Prescott, J (1994) *Sustaining UK food production and our countryside. Centenary College Lecture, Wye College.* Wye College: Occasional Paper No. 94/2.

Rackham, O (1986) *A history of the countryside.* London and Melbourne: J M Dent.

REAG (1992) *Renewable Energy Advisory Group Report to the President of the Board of Trade.* Energy Paper 60. London: Department of Trade and Industry.

Robinson, N (Ed) (1994) *Agenda 21. Earth's Action Plan.* New York, London, Rome: Oceana.

Tolba, M K, El Kholy, O, El Hinnawi, E, Holdgate, M W, McMichael, D F & Munn, R E (Eds) (1992) *The world environment, 1972-1992.* London: Chapman and Hall.

UK (1994a) *Sustainable development: the UK Strategy.* Cm 2426. London: HMSO.

UK (1994b) *Biodiversity. The UK Action Plan.* Cm2428. London: HMSO.

Whitmore, T C, Turner, B L, Johnson, D L, Kates, R W & Gottschang, TR (1990) Long-term population change. In: Turner, B L *et al* (Eds). *The earth as transformed by human action.* Cambridge: University Press.

World Commission on Environment and Development (1987) *Our common future.* Oxford: University Press.

DISCUSSION

Mr Richard Knight (Farming and Wildlife Advisory Group) said that he was pleased that Sir Martin had recognised the valuable contributions made by FWAG, but expressed concern that he had appeared to separate innate conservation issues from what he would describe as forward-looking agriculture. He asked whether the approach advocated was a carrying forward of extensification or a combination of environmental possibilities, as put forward in an earlier paper, that would result in an agriculture which is competitive in world markets and which not only protects the environment but also provides nature conservation benefits.

Sir Martin Holdgate in reply said that as a believer in seeking the best of all possible worlds, he certainly did not want to give the impression that he was other than personally committed to pressing for environmental and agricultural policies to come together. He was sure that landscapes must be looked at area by area to decide the optimum pattern of uses of land and he recognised that this is an approach towards which FWAG can effectively contribute. He was optimistic that this can be done so long as the extraneous variables do not become too great - whether they are environmental variables like climate change, the effect on photosynthesis of ultra-violet penetrations through a thinned ozone screen, or socio-economic variables such as the very real imperatives that will have to be faced world-wide through efforts to promote global sustainability, especially in areas that are going to find it very difficult to feed their own people within their frontiers.

Mrs Vera Chaney (Green Network) commented that when the public object to the distribution of subsidies to farmers, this does not mean that they are not supporting farmers - they are actually supporting small farmers but are very much against the large subsidies being paid to the large farmers.

Ms Annabel Holt (Annabel's Crusade for the Environment) added her concern that although financial support is intended to limit surplus output and conserve wildlife and habitats, every effort should be made to persuade public opinion that in the interests of future generations, such payments should not be regarded as encouragement for the destruction on our living planet of animal and plant life in any form, and that species once lost cannot be re-created.

Sir Martin Holdgate's response was that we should be endeavouring to get the best blend and balance of policies, and that we should accept that this country and all countries in Europe must have highly productive and prosperous agricultural communities. He felt unable to share the wholesale condemnation of the big farmer, nor the wholesale exaltation of the small farmer. He favoured a blend of both within which people can make a decent living and gain personal satisfaction out of farming, even from holdings of modest size. He felt that there are areas where large-scale agriculture is clearly right, and that what is required is a blend of subsidisation that achieves the social goals of the community. On the second point, he was unable to share the condemnation of shooting by proper competent expert shots. He considered that the sustainable use of wildlife control is a legitimate activity and whilst he did not condone inhumanity in any form, he could not go so far as to condemn reasonably competent shooting practices.

Mr Robin Campbell (Farmway) welcomed acceptance by Sir Martin of the necessity for getting the implementation of national strategy down to the local level, and asked him to continue to encourage this approach, especially in the interests of the many people now doing worthwhile work with inadequate recognition. He instanced his own experience of judging the Silver Lapwing Competition, and encouraged all present to look round themselves and see the enormous amount of work being done by small and large individual farmers towards the diversity of conservation work within the community. He expressed particular concern about the damage and stress to local effort by major projects such as National Grid pylons and road development schemes.

Sir Martin Holdgate expressed considerable sympathies with these problems and said that some of the onus does rest on the farming community, in partnership with the conservation community. He believed that that partnership is strong and growing in many areas, and urged publicity to encourage others to set up similar models. Sir Martin also referred to a conference in Manchester last year called 'Partnerships for Change' which was designed to bring together case studies where different sectors of the community had worked through partnerships towards sustainable development. Some very good examples were identified and published, and other participants were inspired to go away and establish working relationships in their fields of interest with the support of broad-based partnerships.

Mrs Ruth Rawling (Cargill Europe) asked Professor Anderson in relation to his world scenario up to 2030 to indicate in more detail whether he expected the increases in productivity to come from Europe, the United States of America or from the former Soviet Union and Asia.

Professor Anderson said that the question was a deeply meaningful one which basically required exposure of the complexities of the model he had used as a basis for summarising. Broadly however he saw the productivity gains as literally across the board, in some parts greater than in others. He referred to earlier references to the likelihood that the higher productivity gains are more likely to come from the relatively good quality agricultural areas rather than from marginal lands, and added that in proportional terms there is a lot more marginal land around, and small productivity gains from these areas which includes the vast tracts of the former Soviet Union will still contribute greatly in the aggregate. His broad assessment was that increased productivity may come from pretty well everywhere with some concentration on the currently most productive lands, and he expected that maize will be the leading commodity.

Ms Annabel Holt (Annabel's Crusade for the Environment) referred to Professor Anderson's analysis of the resources that support agriculture, in particular the 'knowledge' resource, and questioned in the context of DNA genetics of diverse animal and plant life, the value attached by humans to monetary projects and the industrial creation of lifeless and 'soon-to-be-obsolete' machines and objects.

Professor Jock Anderson felt that Sir Martin Holdgate was better equipped to address this question which he interpreted as implying that 'present' people are not as important as 'future' people, and that money is somehow contaminating and dirty, and unnecessary and complicating. As a 'world banker' however he regarded 'today' as probably a bit more important than 'tomorrow' so it would be very distracting to look only to the millenia hence rather the many contemporary problems that have to be addressed very urgently. He also referred to a question raised earlier on the issue of who is going to finance the reforming processes in the countries of Eastern Europe and the former Soviet Union; and he commented that whilst the World Bank will not itself finance the re-structuring, the Bank along with other international agencies, will certainly be a major player.

Sir Martin Holdgate added that it is in his view right that the big strategies like Agenda 21 do stress the importance of the inter-generational equity, rather than passing the world on in a diminished state to future generations. He considered that the achievement of sustainability is not solely a matter of technology, nor a matter of having the money for investment - it is, as is widely recognised in UN agencies and elsewhere, the promotion of good governance in many parts of the world that is an essential part of this whole process. Many countries which expropriated individual and community rights in the belief that the ownership of land should be vested in the State, are now feeling their way back towards restoring rights in land in recognition of the fact that security of tenure provides incentives to care for the land and pass it on in good condition to future generations. Sir Martin also referred to a theme expressed at a meeting in UN headquarters in New York that the amount of money that is wasted by investment in military hardware, even by very impoverished countries, and which is neither used or needed as a deterrent or required for real security, is appalling. There is thus a huge waste of human, financial, technical and material resources which he believed, without being too passionate or anti-military, the world community should consider with a view to redressing the balance through changes of deployment of resources, including greater emphasis on investment in sustainable agricultural developments.

Mr Barry Higgs (Fertilizer Manufacturers Association) expressed his concern about the differences of approach between Professor Anderson and Sir Martin Holdgate in relation to the utilisation of land to feed the increasing world population. He considered that if the world is going to make the most of its soils, then it will need to adopt proper fertiliser practices to improve soil fertility that becomes heavily depleted by 'slash and burn' and various other mining and similar activities; but those in the developed areas with a recognition of this issue appear to be frequently challenged by the philosophies of people who are well-intentioned, but who do not understand the need to replace soil nutrients when they are taken off in the crop.

Sir Martin Holdgate said in response that he believes he is right in saying that 'slash and burn' which we use as a pejorative term need not be a destroyer of fertility. The issue is whether there is enough time for natural processes to restore the soil at the end of the period of cultivation. Whilst he in no way denied the need for proper applications of fertiliser to maintain soil fertility, there are he felt examples where it can be shown that the application of less fertiliser in conjunction with other kinds of husbandry techniques, would not sufficiently diminish yield, and would deliver a net benefit. He finally mentioned examples from Indonesia where as he understood it, substantial sums of money were saved without significant pest infestation problems by adopting fewer pesticide applications in conjunction with integrated pest control processes, including cultivation practices which must be economically much more attractive in developing countries. Though he could not say that there is no justification for the application of fertilisers he felt that it is, as always, a matter of balance.

Professor Jock Anderson, who was invited to make a final comment, said that the only qualifier is that under the population growth scenario he had presented earlier, the intensification of traditional systems like 'slash and burn' is such that they do result in serious destruction of soil fertility, and under such pressures there is no opportunity for nature to take its course in the way that it once did. He felt that systems are no longer sustainable under such intensification and that it is necessary to bring in outside inputs to make them more sustainable.

Marshall BJ & Miller FA (Eds)(1995) *Priorities for a new century - agriculture, food and rural policies in the European Union.* CAS Paper 31. Reading: Centre for Agricultural Strategy.

4 Changes in the pattern of world trade in agricultural products

Michael Davenport

INTRODUCTION

Patterns of trade in agriculture, as in any other sector, can change rapidly and unpredictably. Of course the direction and impact of technological change is of its nature hard to anticipate. But even if agricultural technology were to remain constant over the next two decades, one can be sure that the pattern of world trade in agricultural products would not remain unchanged. On the demand side, the structure of consumer demand will change as personal incomes rise and tastes evolve. On the supply side, technology will develop including fertiliser and pesticide use, biotechnology and so on. But also farmers' responses to price signals, from wherever they come, can be rapid, and given the plethora of other factors that determine farmers' behaviour, they would be hard to forecast, even if the price signals themselves could be predicted. Just as important as any of these factors, agricultural policies will evolve in response to the influence of different lobby groups, consumers, the food industry, other industries using agricultural products as inputs and of course, the farmers themselves.

These developments will all contribute to changes in the prices of different products on the world market and to changes in the pattern of trade flows. I am not planning to offer a comprehensive forecast of all these developments, even for one product, let alone agricultural output in general. What I shall do is less ambitious. I shall discuss some of the reasons why we can be fairly confident that, whatever the patterns of world trade in agriculture in twenty years' time, they will be very different from those of today - in particular, I will concentrate on two of the most important factors. Firstly the re-establishment of market disciplines for the agricultural sector, not only in the western developed countries but also in the Third World, and secondly, the distinct but closely related liberalisation of international trade in agricultural products. I will confine my remarks to temperate agricultural products. Tropical agriculture operates in a more liberal trading environment. The Uruguay Round has more or less removed the few remaining tariffs on unprocessed tropical products, including coffee and cocoa beans, but it is important to remember that there still remains a serious problem of tariff escalation in tropical products. Increasingly higher tariff barriers are imposed by the developed countries as the products become more processed. This obviously makes the development of downstream industries, such as coffee roasting, powdered coffee, cocoa butter and powder production or chocolate much more difficult for the country producing the raw beans. But this is another question. I shall concentrate on temperate agricultural products, which in any event are several times more important than tropical products for the developing countries as a whole, both in production and in consumption. First it is useful to establish the overall structure of world agricultural output and trade.

WORLD AGRICULTURE - THE BROAD PICTURE
There are a number of problems peculiar to agriculture. They differ from country to country. For example in some countries including the southern European Union states, the sector suffers from a relative lack of education, that is human capital. In many countries there is frequently a shortage of non-human capital. Farms are too small and there is insufficient capital equipment. But there are two problems that have combined to create enormous economic and political problems in virtually all the developed countries. These are the combination of declining relative demand and the misguided efforts by governments in the policies they have adopted to support farmers' incomes. On the one hand, as people get richer they spend a lower and lower proportion of their income on food, which means that farm incomes, if left to the market, tend to fall below incomes in the other sectors of the economy. On the other hand, the policy response has traditionally been to artificially support the prices received by the farmer with the result that surpluses are produced which have been dumped on world markets, thereby depressing world market prices.

Of course there are lots of counter-examples. There are agricultural products for which the income elasticity of demand is high - winter fruits and vegetables for example - and also there have been many examples of farm support programmes which have not been based on artificially propping up prices. There are also serious problems with the agricultural policies of the developing countries, which tend to favour urban spending power at the expense of rural incomes - about which I shall have more to say later. However, the characterisation of the predicament of world agriculture as the result of declining relative demand and misguided policies to protect farmers' incomes remains broadly valid. The result has been the expansion of output in the developed countries beyond that which can be utilised and the subsidised export - or dumping - of the excess on world markets.

Table 4.1 gives three measures of the performance of the agricultural sector in the developed countries - that is the western market economies, roughly coextensive with membership of the OECD. It shows how the self-sufficiency ratios, that is the ratio of production to utilisation, and the shares of these countries in world trade have evolved over the period since the early 1960s. Incidentally, the use of the self-sufficiency ratio has no prescriptive connotations. It is just a good measure of the change in the relationship between production

Table 4.1
Self-sufficiency ratios and shares in world trade, developed countries, selected periods[1]

Developed Market Economies	Wheat	Coarse grains	Meat 'red'	Other meat	Dairy products	Sugar
Self-sufficiency						
1961-64	146	98	97	100	104	63
1980-83	195	110	102	100	109	95
1991-93	163	111	103	101	118	104
Share of world exports						
1961-64	83	65	56	78	90	12
1980-83	91	79	70	72	94	29
1991-93	86	75	74	67	99	35
Share of world imports						
1961-64	26	77	80	61	64	58
1980-83	17	48	60	63	53	33
1991-93	8	34	63	56	22	33

[1] The self-sufficiency ratio is the ratio of production to utilisation, ie production plus imports minus exports. All calculations in metric tonnes. Trade among the developed countries is included but not intra-EU trade.

Source: Tyers & Anderson for 1961-64 and 1980-83; Davenport for 1991-93 on the basis of FAO and UN data.

and consumption. Because of data limitations, consumption is defined as production less exports plus imports with no adjustment made for changes in stocks.

The production and export of agricultural goods by the developed market economies expanded greatly in the 1960s and 1970s - though it should be stressed that this represents the continuation of a trend that began much earlier. Between 1961-63 and 1979-81 exports from Western Europe expanded by 232% while imports increased by only 60%. Exports from North America increased by 158% while imports increased by only 36% (Johnson, 1991, p.46).

Table 4.1 summarises the trends for each of the main temperate agricultural commodities. It shows how the developed countries expanded output relative to consumption up to the early 1980s, in all sectors other than 'other meats', which are pigmeat and poultry. In dairy products the trend has continued up to the 1990s, but in general there has been a levelling off of the self-sufficiency ratio, or even a sharp fall in the case of wheat. Outside of wheat and sugar, however, the increase in the self-sufficiency ratio between the early 1960s and the early 1980s seems quite small. Nevertheless the effects on shares in world exports and/or imports were in some cases large, as with coarse grains, ruminant (red) meats and dairy products. In the early 1960s to the early 1980s, the developed countries raised their share of world exports of red meats from 56 to 70%. By now it is about 75%. In the case of dairy products the developed countries now virtually monopolise world exports. In the case of sugar their share rose from 12 to 29% between the early 1960s and the early 1980s. Since then it has gone on up to 35%.

Meanwhile the shares of imports of the developed countries have fallen and this trend has continued through the 1980s in all the main temperate products except in sugar where it appears to have stabilised. Even where there have been significant increases in demand, for example for beef in Japan, that has generally been met by exports from the developed countries, in that particular case from Australia.

The consequences of these trends are shown in more detail in Table 4.2. This gives a snapshot of the self-sufficiency ratios for the European Union(EU), the United States(US), the developed countries as a group and the developing countries as a group. The developed countries now produce substantial surpluses of grains and dairy products and smaller surpluses of meats and sugar. Meanwhile the developing countries and the countries of Eastern Europe and the former Soviet Union are net importers of all these products except sugar. In the case of sugar the former eastern bloc has been a major net importer, largely from Cuba though it is now finding cheaper suppliers, including, I hardly need say, subsidised exports from the EU.

Table 4.2
Self-sufficiency ratio and trade shares for EU, US, developed, developing and countries in transition, 1991-93

1991-93	Wheat	Coarse grains	Meat 'red'	Other meat	Dairy products	Sugar[2]
Self-sufficiency						
European Union	127	107	111	94	120	124
United States	218	127	105	103	102	74
Developed countries	163	111	103	101	118	104
Developing countries	81	93	98	99	66	109
E.Europe and former USSR	84	92	100	99	96	67
Share of world exports						
European Union[1]	20	10	20	13	48	22
United States	33	55	10	19	7	2
Developed countries	86	75	74	67	99	35
Developing countries	12	23	23	33	1	65
E.Europe and former USSR	2	2	3	0	0	1
Share of world imports						
European Union[1]	1	3	4	47	4	12
United States	0	0	1	7	3	10
Developed countries	8	34	63	56	22	33
Developing countries	70	50	33	42	73	46
E.Europe and former USSR	22	16	4	2	6	21

Notes:[1] Intra-EU trade is excluded.
[2] In the case of sugar, data refer to North America rather than the United States.

Source: Author

The other main effect of the agricultural policies of the developed countries on world markets has been to reduce world market prices. This too has had important results for the rest of the world. Incentives for farmers in the developing countries have been diminished and furthermore the import bill for temperate agricultural products for food importing countries has been cut. I will come back to both these issues in due course. But first it is useful to consider the nature of the Uruguay Round agreement.

THE URUGUAY ROUND AGREEMENT ON AGRICULTURE
During the course of the seven years of negotiations, which seemed at the time interminable, certain farmers' groups and sympathetic politicians - not on the whole in the United Kingdom - argued that the effects of the agreement would be seriously detrimental to farming in

Western Europe and North America. Among the western developed countries, only Australia and New Zealand, who had to a large extent eliminated their farm subsidy programmes, were unequivocally in favour of a radical, far-reaching deal. Now, after the Round has reached an agreement, it has been widely denounced or greeted, depending on your viewpoint, as largely irrelevant. It is true the agreement had much of its teeth drawn - the most radical reforms have been watered down and a lot of what is left has been achieved already. Nevertheless I shall argue that it is still going to result in far-reaching changes in the pattern of world agricultural production and trade.

First it may be useful to recapitulate the bare bones of the agreement. The principal decisions were:

- domestic support to the agricultural sector as a whole is to be reduced by 20% over the six-year implementation period, subject to a number of exclusions, including environmental payments and general agricultural development services, and deficiency payments, 'decoupled' from production decisions;
- export subsidies are to be reduced to a level 36% below the 1986-1990 base and the quantity of subsidised exports by 21%, both over the same implementation period;
- non-tariff border barriers - including the levies used to sustain the Common Agricultural Policy (CAP) - are to be replaced by tariffs. Initially the tariffs will provide substantially the same level of protection but they are to be reduced by an average 36% with a minimum reduction of 15% for each tariff line over six years;
- these reductions in import barriers are qualified by a safeguards mechanism. This permits additional tariffs in the event of a major reduction in import prices, or a major increase in import volumes, compared with the base period. The amount of additional duty is determined on a sliding scale, between the actual import price and a reference price;
- finally minimum access tariff quotas (at reduced tariff rates) are established where current imports constitute less than 3% of domestic consumption. These quotas are to be expanded to 5% over the implementation period.

Special provisions were made for the developing countries, both in respect of the implementation period - generally extended to 10 years - and with respect to the extent of liberalisation required.

The lobbyists against liberalisation succeeded in having these measures watered down in several respects:

- instead of the 1986-1990 base period for measuring the required annual changes for reducing subsidised exports, the period 1991-1992 could be used. This so-called front loading means that where the total subsidies were higher in the period 1991-1992, that period could be used as a base to smooth the process of reduction. But it also has the effect of slowing down the adjustment;

- certain policy instruments were excluded from the rules on reduction in domestic supports, ie they were put in the 'green box', even though they could not be said to strictly meet the criterion for the 'green box' which is that they should not be linked to output. In particular the US deficiency payments scheme and the EU's compensation scheme for cereal producers were allowed. In both these schemes, payments are based mainly on historical acreage and yields, but over time improvements in yields can justify increased payments at a later date.

Assessment of results

The typical reaction now is that the package will have very modest effects on world prices and the pattern of trade in those goods where protection among the western industrialised countries has been substantial - grains, (in particular wheat), 'red' meats (beef and sheepmeat), dairy products and sugar. The agreement will lead to a small reduction in exports of these products by the western countries. This will mean that world prices will rise modestly relative to what they would otherwise have been. This assessment certainly underestimates the significance of the Uruguay Round agreement for a number of reasons:

- it takes a minimalist definition of what the Uruguay Round actually achieved in terms of reforms of agricultural policies;
- secondly, if we just take those modest effects on world prices, they can be significant for certain countries including a number of developing countries who could find that their products are competitive, or could be made competitive, on the world market;
- thirdly, it ignores the impact of the Uruguay Round in giving momentum to - even making fashionable - the liberalisation of agricultural trade and, indeed, the liberalisation of trade barriers in general. It is undoubtedly the case that the Uruguay Round has led to the questioning of traditional protectionist dogmas in many countries, in particular, but by no means exclusively, the developing countries. It has also led to the growth of a lobby for the further liberalisation of the agricultural sector - and specifically of agricultural trade - in most developed economies. The momentum for further reform in the CAP is particularly evident.

What to include in an assessment of the Uruguay Round

I shall take each of these points in turn. Firstly in assessing the results of the agricultural side of the Uruguay Round agreement, it is necessary to decide what to include as part of that agreement. Those who pooh-pooh it as not very significant, generally exclude from consideration the 1992 CAP reforms, the so-called MacSharry reforms, as well as the various changes in the US in favour of supply management in place of price supports. In both cases a wide array of measures has been adopted which 'de-couple' subsidies from output. The most obvious of these measures are 'Set-aside' schemes. In some cases where the amount of subsidy is still primarily based on the level of output, the guaranteed price progressively declines beyond a certain level of aggregate output.

One of the reasons for dismissing the effects of the Uruguay Round is based on the fact that many of the requirements, particularly those of reducing domestic subsidies, have already been largely satisfied. For example, the reductions in subsidies to grain production alone in the EU are sufficient to meet the Uruguay Round requirements of a 20% overall cut in agricultural subsidies. But the point is that some of the reforms that have taken place in the EU, the US and elsewhere are attributable to the Uruguay Round, and even where reforms would have taken place in any event, usually because of budgetary pressures, the nature of those reforms, the emphasis on de-coupling subsidies from output, owes a lot to the simultaneous negotiations going on under the Uruguay Round.

Estimates of the Uruguay Round effects
In a recent study I did with the Overseas Development Institute we had access to the OECD RUNS model - RUNS stands for Rural-Urban North-South. The model disaggregates agricultural production and trade into 13 commodity groups and into 22 countries and regions. (It is a general equilibrium model with labour inputs and investment in each sector endogenous, though for each country or region net international capital flows were constrained to predetermined, generally expanding, paths over the ten-year simulation horizon. For details see Golden *et al*, (1993). We simply simulated the Final Act requirements at face value, taking the average required changes in border protection and domestic subsidies and applying them to the base period levels. At first glance the results were quite modest. The price changes derived from the simulation were as follows:

- wheat   3.6%
- rice   0.9%
- coarse grains   1.9%
- sugar   7.9%
- beef, veal and sheep meat   3.7%
- other meats   0.5%

Where protection by the industrialised countries is low and/or their share in world trade is low, the final price effect will be low. This tends to be the case for rice and other meats. Where the opposite situation prevails, in sugar and dairy goods, the price effects tend to be at the top of the range. For grains and red meats they were in the middle.

These are the final, 'steady state', effects. They measure the differences between the projected price levels absent from the Uruguay Round agreement with those taking account of the Round, after all the lags have worked out. These price changes are modest compared with some of the numbers which have been produced (see Page *et al*, 1991). But even these changes in the world market will be of real significance to particular countries. Take for example sugar. The Uruguay Round agreement is specifically devoid of teeth as regards sugar. The EU is the largest exporter other than Cuba, whose particular problems are acute and critical to the future of the world sugar market but are a separate issue from that of the Uruguay Round. But the EU is also a major importer. The suppliers are those African, Caribbean and Pacific countries who are listed in the Sugar Protocol to the Lomé Convention. They are allowed to export specific quotas of cane sugar to the EU, which means in practice the UK, and receive for these prices close to the EU intervention price.

The impact of the agreement on the EU's sugar régime will be considerably delayed. The EU can avoid major changes for at least four years, firstly, because it can use the price of imports of Protocol sugar as its base import price despite the fact that that was several times the world price at the time. The EU will then be able to impose safeguard tariffs on imports from the rest of the world. At any plausible world prices, these tariffs will be sufficient to prevent any forced reduction in the intervention price as a result of tariffication and the scheduled reductions in tariffs. Secondly, the targets for reducing the volumes of subsidised EU sugar exports will be radically eased by the admission of four new 'sugar deficit' members from EFTA (European Free Trade Association) and rising EU consumption. Thirdly, the flexible implementation over the six years of the reductions in the volumes of subsidised exports and expenditures on export subsidies means that, if, as is likely, the Commission decides to 'play by ear' in setting annually the intervention price and the levels of the A and B sugar output quotas, it should be able to avoid any significant cuts in these until the year 1999. Nevertheless, the eventual effects on the world sugar price, though they could be concentrated in 1999 and 2000, could be as much as 7 or 8%.

As long as the price paid for ACP (Africa, the Caribbean and the Pacific) sugar remains tied to the EU intervention price, the ACP sugar producers will experience cuts in their export earnings. We expect a reduction of EU intervention prices of 10-12%. On the other hand, the rise in world prices may allow certain ACP producers, including Jamaica, to sell on the world market. The most efficient estate factory in Jamaica, Worthy Park, can produce sugar at approximately 13-14 cents per lb. The production cost of the least efficient is now some 17-18¢. The current world price is some 12¢ plus, though this has been boosted by drought in some major growing countries. There will be upward pressures on the world price from the Uruguay Round agreement and 7-8% was suggested earlier. There will of course be many other factors affecting the world price. Increased output in Eastern Europe and the former Soviet Union will have a negative effect. On the other hand, the world price should be strengthened by the diversification out of sugar production of Cuba, which is the world's largest exporter but one that is generally uncompetitive at world prices. In any event the potential competitiveness of Jamaican sugar on the world market within several years will be given a significant, and perhaps critical, boost by the Uruguay Round.

For the first time in many decades, Jamaica may be able to sell sugar on the world market - at least that produced by its most competitive estates. Now it can sell only on the EU market where prices paid are similar to those received by EU sugar-beet growers. In due course, with more investment in plant and irrigation, some of the other estates may also become competitive in the world market. This could be critical for Jamaica, since there must be a big question mark over the future of special access that the EU grants to Caribbean sugar - or, indeed, other ACP agricultural products - beyond the present Lomé Convention which expires in the year 2000.

Table 4.3 shows estimates using the RUNS model of the effects on the self-sufficiency ratio for the EU, the US, and developed, developing and East European groups. It also gives the results for a number of individual countries and other country groupings. It shows that there will be significant reductions in the self-sufficiency ratio in most products in the case of the EU, the US and, largely as a result, the developed countries as a group. There will be corresponding increases in the ratios for the developing countries and, except for 'other' meats, the transition countries of Eastern Europe and the former Soviet Union.

When we look at the more detailed results for individual countries and country groups, we see that there will be major effects in China across the board. Output of dairy products and sugar, in particular, will be boosted in India and the low income Asian countries. The effects on Indonesia are substantial for most commodities. In the case of Africa, the production of dairy products in particular will be boosted. Part of the reason for the effects on Africa being generally small is the dispensations from liberalisation given to the least developed countries. So whether Africa will join in the movement towards liberalisation remains to be seen. At the moment, farmers in many countries of sub-Saharan Africa are the victims of policies designed to supply cheap food to the urban population.

Table 4.3
Estimates of effects of Uruguay Round on self-sufficiency ratios

1991-93	Wheat	Coarse grains	Meat 'red'	Other meat	Dairy products	Sugar
European Union	-4.0	-9.7	-10.8	-0.5	-6.4	-17.8
United States	-14.3	-4.8	-2.0	-0.4	-6.7	-8.2
Developed countries	-6.6	-0.8	-5.7	-1.2	-6.7	-11.6
Developing countries	1.6	0.2	4.2	1.8	5.2	4.2
E.Europe and former USSR	0.3	1.2	1.3	-2.8	3.8	-2.2
Low Inc. Asia[1]	2.5	3.1	2.5	1.0	4.8	6.7
China	2.9	2.9	11.0	2.3	9.0	7.7
India	1.2	1.8	3.9	0.1	6.2	8.2
Upper Inc. Asia[2]	0.0	-8.2	-4.5	1.8	-1.5	-7.7
Indonesia	0.0	5.0	4.0	5.0	5.9	-3.4
Africa[3]	0.6	1.0	3.9	1.1	5.0	-2.1
Nigeria	-0.5	2.7	5.0	2.1	3.2	1.1
South Africa	1.1	-1.3	-0.7	-1.6	-1.2	-15.5
Maghreb[4]	0.1	-0.8	6.8	3.2	0.1	6.9
Mediterranean[5]	0.9	1.0	4.8	2.0	4.2	-2.7
Gulf[6]	-2.0	-1.0	-3.2	-12.5	0.4	-1.8
Latin America[7]	3.2	1.2	3.3	1.3	5.3	4.8
Brazil	-2.4	-4.2	6.5	3.8	8.5	11.6
Mexico	-2.4	-4.0	12.5	-3.4	4.9	6.9
Canada	3.3	1.3	-5.9	-2.9	-6.6	0.2
Australia, New Zealand	5.5	3.0	6.0	-0.5	-2.2	19.5
Japan	-3.4	-0.2	-8.7	-4.8	-11.5	-4.5
EFTA	-10.3	0.2	-15.1	-12.9	-6.8	-13.2

Notes:
[1] Afghanistan, Bangladesh, Bhutan, Burma, Kampuchea, Korea (DR), Laos, Maldives, Mongolia, Nepal, Pakistan, Sri Lanka, Vietnam
[2] Brunei, Fiji, Fr. Polynesia, Hong Kong, Korea (rep), Macao, Malaysia, New Caledonia, New Hebrides, Papua New Guinea, Philippines, Singapore, Taiwan, Thailand, Tonga
[3] Sub-Saharan Africa less South Africa
[4] Algeria, Morocco, Tunisia
[5] Cyprus, Egypt, Israel, Jordan, Lebanon. Libya, Malta, Syrian Arab Rep., Turkey
[6] Bahrain, Iraq, Iran (IR of), Kuwait, Oman, Qatar, Saudi Arabia, UAE, Yemen (Arab Rep. of), Yemen (PDR)
[7] excluding Brazil and Mexico

Source: Author

Most frequently farmers are required to sell their output at arbitrary, and generally low, prices to marketing boards. Their incentives to invest in cultivating new land or increasing yields are minimal.

Table 4.3 shows that the Uruguay Round will encourage output of particular products in particular areas. For example in the Maghreb and the Mediterranean the main opportunities will come in meat, while in Latin America they will come in dairy products and sugar. For Latin America there will be also new or restored opportunities to export meat. Table 4.3 shows Mexico and Brazil with major increases in their self-sufficiency ratios, but other producers in that region will also gain. In some cases earlier export flows may be restored, for example trade between different parts of Africa in beef which has been destroyed by cheap beef exports from the EU.

If it is likely that the EU will reach a rough balance in the red-meat sector, if not indeed once again become a net importer, the question of grains is more controversial. Some people argue that after the fall in output brought about by the Set-aside programme, output will recover with steady productivity gains of 1-2% per year, and this will not create a problem in meeting Uruguay Round requirements as it will be competitive on world markets without subsidies. I find this unconvincing as it fails to take account of the greater opportunities for productivity growth in certain other regions, in particular the Third World and the former Eastern bloc. These results are based on one model and subject to wide margins of uncertainty. I do not present them as reliable predictions of the effects of the GATT Agreement, but simply as illustrative of the sort of changes that could occur when relatively small price changes are transmitted to the agricultural sector and are allowed to determine production decisions.

As I suggested before, attitudes to the farm sector in the developing countries are changing. There is now a much greater willingness to allow world price movements to influence farmers' decisions. The insulation of the agricultural sector from the outside world through taxes on exports, tariffs on imports, administered prices and other interventions in the market has in many countries been significantly reduced, and in others is being seriously examined. This means that farmers in the developing countries will increasingly have the incentive to respond to world price signals, both as regards the particular commodities they produce and the quantities in which they produce them. Some commentators (eg, Madden & Madeley, 1993) have argued that the developing countries as a whole, and the poorest in particular, will be damaged by the Uruguay Round agreement because they are net food importers and the price of food is likely to rise with the implementation of the agreement. This is true, but as I emphasise, the agricultural sectors in the developing countries will have further incentive to increase their own production if the rise in world prices is passed through. We calculate that the negative effects will be small. In the case of Africa, the poorest region and that most dependent on food imports, net imports of temperate foodstuffs will increase by 4.5%.

Some or maybe all of that negative effect could be offset by policies designed to encourage food production - or the elimination of existing anti-farm trade and tax policies. Incidentally, in the 1960s Africa was a net exporter of food.

Of course in the end, supply and demand under the Uruguay Round régime must balance. Aggregate agricultural sales in the EU, Japan and EFTA will be reduced, but that does not mean that farm incomes will necessarily suffer. That depends on the various schemes for decoupled assistance among which, as we have seen, the EU compensation payments and US deficiency payments schemes are included. It also depends on whether the farmers in the developed market economies can continue, or, in some cases, go back to, safeguarding their real disposable incomes through reducing input costs and raising labour productivity. They too, in a number of sectors may be able to sell without subsidy on the world market, as presently happens in some EU member states with C quota sugar.

THE MOMENTUM FOR REFORM

The momentum for more reform is probably unstoppable. True, there are other factors such as the importance of extending membership to the countries of Central Europe - initially Poland, the Czech Republic, Slovakia and Hungary - which would be out of the question because of the budgetary cost to existing member states if the present CAP operating rules were to remain in effect. Germany will continue to press for this because it wants to Europeanise its responsibilities along its eastern border. But even without such special factors, the conviction that the rules that have governed the international trading system as far as industrial products are concerned should be extended to agricultural products - and incidentally, to the other main hitherto excluded textiles and clothing sector - has overwhelmingly won the day. Until the last few years the agricultural sector was, to use deliberately a French phrase, a *chasse gardée*, which could be translated as 'out of bounds' to the GATT and international rules in general'. That is no longer the case.

The new proposals for radical change in the CAP in an independent study *EC Agricultural Policy for the 21st Century* recently published by the European Commission are witness to the momentum for further liberalisation. True, the report was commissioned by DG II - the Directorate for Economic and Financial Affairs as opposed to DG VI, the Directorate for Agriculture in the European Commission - some years ago and the report was finalised, I believe, about two years ago. It has only now been made public. It proposes a flat subsidy to all EU farmers, unrelated to their output, which could be topped up at the member state level and is bound to be resisted. That smacks too much of welfare. But it is consistent with the trend of a shift towards liberalising markets and treating income support as a separate issue - going beyond such policies as Set-aside which still represent major interventions in the market, even if on the supply side. But liberalisation will not be limited to the developed countries. As I have already argued, among the developing countries there is a new commitment to markets and to the role of price signals. After years of preaching by the International Monetary Fund and the World Bank, the Uruguay Round seems to have been the catalyst for their conversion.

The Uruguay Round agreement foresees the start of new negotiations on agriculture before the end of the six-year implementation period. The developing countries are likely to insist that the timetable is met and the negotiations are meaningful and far-reaching. Prior to 1947 the average tariff on non-agricultural goods was over 40%. After seven rounds of multilateral trade negotiations under GATT it was brought down to 5%. With the implementation of the Uruguay Round it will come down to 3.5%. The same sort of progress could be achieved in agriculture, only much faster.

REFERENCES

European Commission Directorate-General for Economic and Financial Affairs (1994) *EC agricultural policy for the 21st century.* European Economy No 4. Brussels: ECSC-EC-EAEC.

Goldin, I, Knudsen, O & van der Mensbrugghe, D (1993) *Trade liberalisation: global economic implications.* Washington & Paris: World Bank & OECD.

Johnson, G D (1991) *World agriculture in disarray.* 2nd Edn. London: Macmillan.

Madden, P & Madeley, J (1993) *Winners and losers: the impact of the GATT Uruguay Round on Developing Countries.* London: Christian Aid.

Page, S, Davenport, M & Hewitt, A (1991) *The GATT Uruguay Round: effects on developing countries.* London: Overseas Development Institute.

Tyers, R & Anderson, K (1986) *Distortions in world food markets; a quantitative assessment.* Background paper for the World Bank's World Development Report 1986. Washington: World Bank.

Marshall BJ & Miller FA (Eds)(1995) *Priorities for a new century -
agriculture, food and rural policies in the European Union.* CAS Paper 31.
Reading: Centre for Agricultural Strategy.

5 Industry response - agricultural production

David Naish

I find myself much in agreement with Dr Davenport's analysis of the
world situation and the pressures that are developing, but as a result of
the deliberations we have had so far, I have tried to consider whether
to allow common sense to triumph over complacency or the reverse,
because we have, I think, been presented with the absolute extremes of
the situations and conditions against which farmers have to take their
decisions.

The most significant UK farming industry response to the CAP
reforms and the GATT settlement has been the launching of a
thoroughgoing debate on the direction in which farmers themselves
want the industry to move. I welcome the opportunity to be part of that
debate through the publication of our own discussion document
entitled *Real choices* (NFU, 1994); appreciation of the impact of the
further enlargement of the European Union (EU) with the addition of
the central European countries has furthermore instigated yet another
National Farmers' Union (NFU) review of how that expansion is likely
to affect the future of our industry. I am convinced that farmers can no
longer sit back and let others determine their future for them and I am
pleased and proud that the NFU was in the vanguard with *Real choices*
which was designed to set out the issues without attempting to reach
conclusions, thus encouraging farmers themselves to participate fully
in the debating process. The document focused the thinking of farmers
in broad terms on the choice between increased reliance on production
restraints, such as milk quotas or land set aside, or ending reliance on
price support through intervention using either bonds or decoupled
payments. More specifically the options offered for consideration are:

- output quotas - for: can control production;
  - against: complicated to administer and can act as a barrier to new entrants;
  - conclusion: they would be impractical.
- bonds   - for: facilitate the rapid restructuring of the EU farming industry to compete in world markets;
  - against: the cost of fully compensating EU farmers would be very high and restructuring could lead to further social costs; to whom would the bonds be paid - landlord or land occupier?;
  - conclusion: too rapid structural changes and high costs would be totally unacceptable to many EU governments.
- input quotas - for: allow prices to be maintained above world levels;
  - against: undermine international competitiveness of agriculture and the food industry;
  - conclusion: could be environmentally friendly and they already exist in the reformed CAP.
- decoupling   - for: reduce the risk of over-production by breaking the link between production and support;
  - against: if farm incomes are to be sustained they could mean higher public costs which would be unattractive to the EU;
  - conclusion: international competitiveness of the food industry would improve and there could be environmental benefits.

My own view, which is wholly in line with Dr Davenport's approach, is that the GATT settlement has created a watershed. The downward pressure on prices and on government support becomes a politically international policy within the EU which now puts a total limit on the amount of export subsidies that any member country can apply. I am sure that at some point (and I recognise that we disagree with Government on precisely when that will be) the capacity of farmers within the Union to increase production will mean that the industry is producing more than can be consumed or permitted to be exported with subsidy. There will then be only two choices - either to restrain support by taking more land out of production through further Set-aside and similar measures like ratcheting back milk quotas; or to bite the bullet and accept that our prices are going to reduce further and further so that we do not need to subsidise exports and then look for some form of decoupled compensation to help us to adjust to the new situation.

I have to say, however, that this choice is no choice. Although the idea of cutting back production to keep up prices has a superficial attraction to many farmers, it offers no long-term future either to them or the industry. The only perspective it offers is ever-increasing rates of Set-aside and further quota cuts as greater productivity increases our output levels, and further GATT rounds increase our imports and further lower our right to subsidise exports. Our costs of production will subsequently increase, we will become less globally competitive, and there will always be a risk that the supply management mechanisms will be biased against the larger structure of agriculture in the UK. (I was however delighted by the Minister's response to a question on this issue, in which he strongly defended the efficient structure of UK agriculture). This kind of policy could furthermore be really dangerous in the context of further enlargement of the EU to include Central and Eastern European countries, since the effect would be to raise farmers' prices, provide signals for increasing production, and prevent them from exporting on to world markets.

The other choice - lower prices and decoupled support mechanisms - is no easy route, especially, for the NFU President in addressing the issue to a farming audience! Much as I would like to think there would be, there can be no guarantee of total compensation as prices come down. Competition would be fierce between farmer and farmer, and country and country, and further structural change would be inevitable largely in Europe, but also in the UK with some loss of farming businesses. I was obviously pleased to hear Commissioner Steichen's report to us that the changes in CAP policies had in the current year achieved a saving of 3 billion ECUs, but I feel this must be seen in the context of strong world markets and a weak US dollar.

So the question that has to be put is where should we be aiming with this option? Our goal should I think be to eliminate Set-aside, recognising of course that this cannot happen overnight. The 3% reduction, which we urged for market reasons, is a useful signal to farmers that no mechanism is set in stone, and its use as a market tool rather than as a long-term measure, encourages me to turn to the sensitive topic of milk quotas. This form of constraint has been generally popular with those who already hold them, but it is becoming evident that some of these farmers are now questionning whether they are in the long-term interest of the UK dairy industry. It is also significant that the NFU Potato Committee now considers that the quota policy accepted in the past may not be in the interests of producers having regard to likely future developments; and similarly in the light of the possible direction of further CAP reforms, the questions are starting to be asked and debated in respect of suckler-cow and ewe quotas.

I have to say that UK farmers are fortunate to be in a relatively good position to confront these very difficult challenges. Their economic position, with the current exception of the pig sector, is good. We have had two years of benefit from the devaluation of sterling and the removal of the green pound, and I believe we can probably look forward to one or two years' breathing space during which we can look closely at the position of our businesses and make certain that we are in a position to compete with the new challenges. May I stress to farmers the vital importance of using that respite wisely, in particular by reducing their input costs, improving their productivity, and by strengthening their position in the agri-food chain.

This new situation brings exciting challenges which we have not had before. We can no longer look at farming in isolation - if we want a competitive industry we must have a competitive food chain. There is still much to be done within the NFU; our objectives will be:-

- to convince farmers that they must strengthen their position in the food chain, forging links upstream and downstream - recognising the needs of their customers and planning their farming businesses accordingly; and developing meaningful partnerships with retailers, caterers and manufacturers;
- to urge the Government to look at all its policies from the standpoint of the competitiveness of the UK farming industry; recognising that the Farm Tenancy Bill and milk deregulation are steps in the right direction, but pressing for more to be done to reduce the burden of legislation and remove unnecessary costs which limit our competitive position across Europe and into world markets generally;
- to encourage greater involvement in the fruits of science and technology through better understanding of the technologies of biotechnology, genetic manipulation, and biodiversity;
- to emphasise the importance of reaction to changing nutritional standards and to the changing market requirements to meet consumer demands and tastes.

Finally I would like to turn to several other policy studies and debates, which are all warmly welcomed by the NFU and which have taken place following the publication of our own *Real choices* report - these are the *EC Agricultural policy for the 21st century* study recently issued after some delay by the European Commission, the Country Landowners' Association (CLA) policy review and recommendations entitled *Focus on the CAP* and the Briefing Paper prepared by a high-level group convened by the European Programme of the Royal Institute of International Affairs (Franklin & Ockenden, 1994) about which we shall be hearing more from Sir Michael Franklin later in the conference.

Firstly, within the EC Report there is a suggestion relating to renationalisation of agricultural policy formulation and I can see that there may be a theoretical call for saying that if aid schemes are decoupled, they do not influence production and can therefore be left to national governments. We must, however, be extremely wary of this argument - in the long-term it may be possible, but in the foreseeable future I am convinced that it is impracticable. We are absolutely clear that there must be a common policy in the EU, the core elements of which must be centrally determined and centrally financed. The examples of some other industries are a ghastly reminder - with the best will in the world (and I am not sure that the Commission has that) it has been impossible to regulate state aids in major industries like steel and the airlines, and we must learn from these mistakes.

The second point that comes through from the EC and CLA reports is that compensation should be degressive - may I just remind this conference that the EU has just signed a GATT agreement that limits the amount that any member country is allowed to pay in subsidy to its farmers, and then reduces this by 20% over the next six years. Further GATT rounds may well impose further cuts. The NFU particularly wants European and UK farming to become globally competitive; however, as most other countries in the world subsidise their agricultural production to some extent, any cuts imposed on European farmers that are not applied in other countries, would create serious risks to our competitive position. Whilst I am willing to discuss multi-lateral cuts I must resist unilateralism in this area.

Finally, I would like to comment on a proposition frequently advocated by environmental and other organisations that much or all financial support should be withdrawn from production and applied to environmental measures. The NFU, as I have already said, is in favour of de-coupling - in other words support should not be provided simply to encourage farmers to increase production by being totally commodity-linked. But it must be realised that farmers are often not just producers of commodities, they are also providers of a service - the visual appearance of the landscape, the protection and care of the environment, and the providers of recreation and tourism facilities which for example in the Lake District are worth £500 million per year. Some farmers may well wish to concentrate on these aspects and since the market cannot reward them, there is a clear case for appropriate forms of public support. The NFU favours this type of transfer of public funds but considers that it should be available generally to all farmers on a first-come first-served menu basis rather than available just to those who happen to farm in particular areas. Such an approach would solve many of the problems inherent in the present plethora of schemes that create confusion of administration and interpretation, and would certainly be more realistic than a policy prescribing that all or most support should be for environmental or rural development purposes which would condemn all farmers to higher costs and a loss of competitiveness.

The primary role for our industry must be the production of high-quality safe products, with proper account being taken of all reasonable environmental constraints that we well recognise will be increasingly placed upon us. Our industry has successfully completed its post World War II contract with the government and taxpayer and is ready to move on to its new wider-based contract of growing and marketing the food in response to the ever-increasing demands of the consumer, marketing the products more effectively, and maintaining the all-important rural infrastructure of which we have reason to be proud. For the foreseeable future such an industry will need some assistance to adapt and become truly competitive on a European and global scale. Our farmers are faced with opportunities they must seize, and I am confident that they will follow the lead that we and others are putting forward to ensure that they meet the challenges and remain market leaders in the world.

REFERENCES

CLA (1994) *Focus on the CAP.* London: CLA.

European Commission Directorate-General for Economic and Financial Affairs (1994) *EC Agricultural policy for the 21st century.* European Economy No 4. Brussels: ECSC-EC-EAEC.

Franklin, M & Ockenden. J. (1994) *European agricultural policy - ten steps in the right direction.* Briefing Paper No 14. London: The Royal Institute of International Affairs.

NFU (1994) *Real choices.* A discussion document by the Long-Term Strategy Group. London: NFU.

Marshall BJ & Miller FA (Eds)(1995) *Priorities for a new century - agriculture, food and rural policies in the European Union.* CAS Paper 31. Reading: Centre for Agricultural Strategy.

6 Industry response - the UK supply and merchanting industry

Martin Lowe

INTRODUCTION

I would like to begin by outlining the functions of the United Kingdom Agricultural Supply Trade Association (UKASTA) which represents the interests of about 400 companies responsible for the vital range of inputs and outputs that are central to the efficient performance of our food production industry (see Table 6.1); and the key developments, many of which have been brought out by previous speakers, that will affect the commercial, technical, financial, and research decisions and directions of our diverse group of member organisations.

Table 6.1
United Kingdom Agricultural Supply Trade Association

Inputs	Outputs
Feed	Crop storage
Seed	Arable marketing
Fertilisers	
Agrochemicals	
Forage additives	

Source: Author

Firstly the tremendous upward trend in world population (see Table 6.2), in particular the significant increases during the period 1980 to 1990 in Africa, South America, Asia and the middle east countries - an average increase of 2% per annum; and secondly productivity increases through more and better management of land, better use of water and

88

Table 6.2
Population trends (millions)

	1980	1990	% Change
World	4450	5288	+19
Africa	481	645	+34
North and Central America	373	428	+15
South America	240	297	+24
Asia	2583	3100	+20
USSR	266	292	+10
Oceania	23	27	+17
Middle East	151	186	+23
Europe	484	497	+3
(EC 12 including former GDR	318	350)	

Source: EURIBRID Holland

other resources, and technological and human capital improvements. Also of significance is the large oversupply, on a global basis, of wheat at about 160% and dairy products at about 120%, the continued urbanisation under which something of the order of 45% of the world's population now live in towns and cities, the falling number of people employed in agriculture (see Table 6.3) (an average downward trend of 5% between 1980 and 1990), the reduction in the average percentage of total income spent on food (see Figure 6.1), and the interesting trend in the indices of deflated retail prices for meat and other food items (see Figure 6.2).

Table 6.3
Population active in agriculture (%)

	1980	1990
World	49	45
Africa	65	61
North and Central America	15	13
Mexico	37	30
USA	4	3
South America	29	24
Brazil	31	24
Asia	63	58
Japan	11	6
China	74	68
Thailand	67	61
USSR	20	13
Oceania	19	17
Middle East	41	32
Europe	13	9
EC 12	9	6
Central	21	15

Source: EURIBRID Holland

Figure 6.1
Average total income spent on food (% all households in UK)

Source: Department of Employment

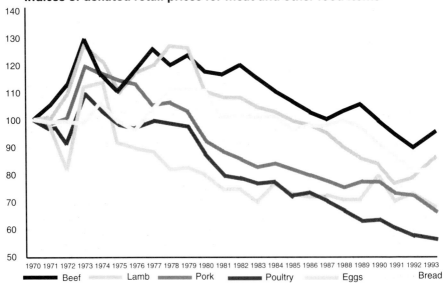

Figure 6.2
Indices of deflated retail prices for meat and other food items

Beef ▬▬▬ Lamb ▬▬▬ Pork ▬▬▬ Poultry ▬▬▬ Eggs ▬▬▬ Bread

Source: Author (based on MLC meat demand trends and other sources)

It is of the utmost importance that our industries closely monitor these and other key trends, and take them fully into account in determining their long-term policies.

MAIN FACTORS LIKELY TO AFFECT UKASTA

I would now like to develop the main factors - market share, information technology, and price volatility - that will in my view affect the organisations within UKASTA.

Increased competition for market share

It is here that political developments have been of greatest significance. CAP reform and the imposition of Set-aside, coupled with the Blair House agreement on oilseeds, cut back at a stroke the amount of seed and fertiliser required in the UK, and the volume of grains and oilseeds to be marketed. These developments left supply and merchanting companies fighting for volume and accelerated a process of rationalisation. For example although we represent no less in terms of total turnover, the number of organisations represented within UKASTA has reduced from 800 in the early 1980s to 400 today. Major companies such as BP have been divesting but there have been no compensation payments for the supply industry to soften the blow.

Policy changes affecting the livestock sector have been no less dramatic and the imposition of milk quotas in 1984 was equally devastating for the feed industry. Now we look forward to more flexibility or even a phasing out of the milk quota system. Meanwhile, competition for market share will intensify. The GATT settlement is another factor driving the reforms. It has begun the process of bringing EU agriculture into the global market, and the industry which has not needed in the past to look beyond the UK, may find that to survive and flourish it has no alternative. The end of the 'cold war' is another factor that is influencing future markets. In its immediate aftermath it caused major disruptions in the fertiliser market and since many of the CEE countries are parties to GATT, we face new competitors in 'our'markets. For example in pigmeat and eggs, substantial imports are predicted by the year 1999.

Information technology and communications

As the policy barriers to a global market come down, technology allows it to function efficiently as one market; and clearly the major development in information technology and communication will revolutionise the way we do business in the new and wider markets and UK market knowledge will in future be tied to international market knowledge.

Price volatility

Concentration of UK and EU free market trade will put greater pressure on ex-farm prices, but as governments withdraw from the management of prices and move towards the management of incomes via direct payments, then price volatility will increase. The nearer EU prices move towards world prices, the more significant this factor will be (see Figure 6.3).

Figure 6.3
US and EU wheat prices converge (dollars per metric tonne)

Source: USDA

Consumer-led specifications

Another important point for the supply industry to acknowledge is that customers now wish, and are able to, specify their requirements much more closely. This includes increasing consumer pressures on governments to prescribe ever more rigorous standards for food health and the environment, of which a good example is the Food Safety Act which is being translated down the food chain from the retailers.

UKASTA'S RESPONSE

Our response to all these developments is three-fold; we need to continue to improve efficiency, to become more expert in controlling quality and prices, and to develop partnerships with our customers and suppliers.

92

Greater efficiency

Improving our efficiency is something we have been doing for a long time - recent CAP reform was not the beginning of cost squeeze for the farmer and supplier but it has intensified the need to control costs. Only the most efficient companies are surviving in the supply trade. CAP reform is likely to reduce crop incomes, leading to ever greater pressure from farmers on input costs. Developments in the fertiliser sector are an example of how greater efficiencies can be brought into play. More product now moves between factory and farm direct.

If a farmer is to incur added cost from a distributor there has to be value added. UKASTA is working with the Fertiliser Manufacturers' Association to improve industry standards in market information, training and marketing. The aim is to make the pricing and sourcing of fertiliser much more understandable and/or provide more advice on its optimum use. In terms of merchanting grain, costs in the UK remain competitive with French costs. It is possible to move grain for $11 a tonne ex-farm to f.o.b. sea vessel. The French cost is similar. Elsewhere, for example in Germany, it is nearly $30 a tonne.

Continuing to improve efficiency in these ways does depend on having a government policy which does not impose unnecessary additional burdens on the industry. We cannot guarantee our competitiveness if we do not have this kind of support, particularly if our competitors in Europe receive such support from their governments.

Risk management

But moving limited volumes of product at ever lower costs is not in itself a recipe for the future of the agricultural supply industry. It is becoming ever more important to be able to deliver a quality product - a product which meets the detailed specification laid down. This is as true for our sales of inputs such as fertiliser, and especially feed, as it is for our sales of outputs. We are working toward a national qualification for sellers of fertiliser. Feed ingredient supply is becoming not just a question of price on the day but also what quality guarantees come with particular ingredients. And at the other end of the supply chain customers want to know exactly where a particular load of grain or oilseeds originated and they are increasingly laying down exact specifications. UKASTA has developed a grain passport system to indicate the pesticide residue status of a crop, in response to customer demands for more information. With the specialised development of alternative crop uses as well, we will be needing more differentiated and specialised storage in future. The information requirement and the need for guarantees will also lead to the development of long-term preferred suppliers.

If governments are moving out of price management - as we have seen in oilseeds and are beginning to see in grain - then there is a vacuum in the management of price risks. Some parts of the merchanting trade have wide experience of markets and methods used to offset price risk such as hedging techniques and options, but they have previously pursued this as a separate activity. In future this will become an integral part of merchanting a farmer's grain and the merchant will have to enable the farmer to understand and use these risk management tools, or gain the farmer's trust in using the tools on his behalf, perhaps including guaranteed minimum prices. The first European oilseed futures market, for rapeseed, has just started up in Paris. Price risks can be managed via such a market but clear advice on exactly what that market can and cannot provide to a farmer must be the first priority.

Partnership
Developing efficiency and the need for risk management lead to the concept of partnership. We are already seeing more vertical integration and more farmers joining together with suppliers. Less and less business will be done 'spot' or between farmers and suppliers and merchants who do not know each other. UKASTA's independent local merchants will have to focus on their local knowledge and strengths in order to continue to compete. Any traditional adversarial attitude between the 'supply trade' and farmers will merge into the common interest to meet future challenges and to:
- expand the local and export markets;
- improve efficiency and safety;
- achieve stability;
- coordinate supplies and manage quality in the food chain;
- preserve and protect the environment.

CONCLUSIONS
May I say in conclusion that those who will survive and progress in the agricultural and food chain will be those who improve efficiency, manage risks, and develop partnerships; and I would add as a final thought that there is no reason why businesses should remain confined to the UK. The skills required will be applicable in the wider marketplace, not only in EU but particularly in eastern Europe; and if we join in partnerships we will need to develop them on a more multinational basis.This offers great opportunities but we have to acknowledge that the farmers' customers today are increasingly the processors and the large purveyors of agricultural produce and the development of these wider markets makes it easier to do business in different localities - for example the food processing companies will

Figure 6.4
UK exports of food, drink and tobacco (includes live animals)

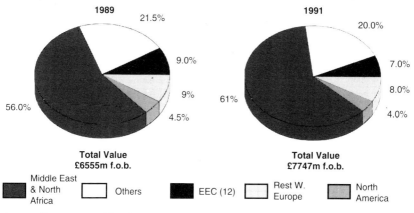

1989

21.5%

9.0%

9%

56.0%

4.5%

Total Value
£6555m f.o.b.

1991

20.0%

7.0%

8.0%

61%

4.0%

Total Value
£7747m f.o.b.

Middle East
& North
Africa

Others

EEC (12)

Rest W.
Europe

North
America

Source: Department of Employment

Figure 6.5
The food chain

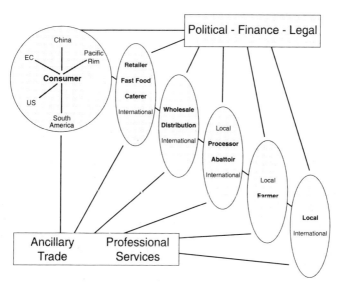

Political - Finance - Legal

China

EC

Pacific
Rim

Retailer

Consumer

Fast Food

Caterer

US

International

South
America

Wholesale

Distribution

International

Local

Processor

Abattoir

International

Local

Farmer

Local

International

Ancillary
Trade

Professional
Services

Source: P. Holroyd Associates

95

tend to locate their plants to achieve maximum efficiency and benefits from the areas of production of their appropriate crop and livestock raw material. This trend will furthermore provide opportunities for exports. Figure 6.4 indicates the value and destinations of our export trade for the short period 1989 to 1991 and provides the challenge for even greater success in the future.

Achievement of this success depends on our recognition of how we can most effectively fit into the global food chain (see Figure 6.5), since that is where the future undoubtedly lies in effective linkages from the farm right through to the consumer.

Marshall BJ & Miller FA (Eds)(1995) *Priorities for a new century - agriculture, food and rural policies in the European Union.* CAS Paper 31. Reading: Centre for Agricultural Strategy.

7 Industry response - agricultural crop protection

Don Taylor

INTRODUCTION

As we look ahead to the problems and prospects of the next thirty years, may I take as my starting point the key question posed, and to some extent analysed by Professor Jock Anderson - 'will mankind have sufficient food available to meet the large projected increase in population?' With very little additional land available for food production, and world population set to double, the need for intensive farming seems self-evident. Unless we are to see a new world order, with the developed world sharing more of its food resources, then the focus in the developed world will be on **quality**, and in the developing world on **quantity** (see Figure 7.1).

FUTURE OF AGRICULTURE

So, in the global context in which the agrochemicals industry must address its future role and the nature and direction of its research and investment, there is a further significant question that needs to be asked: 'Can technology and science bridge the gap between today's food production and the requirements of the world population in the future?'. To answer this vital question it is worth looking at the track record of the last thirty years or so and then at the likely technological breakthroughs over the next forty years.

An analysis of the extent to which farming has increased its productivity (see Figure 7.2) shows that at the turn of the 19th century and up to the beginning of the 20th century, the European farmer was just about feeding his own family of two or three people, with no dramatic increase until 1950, and then rising by 1990 to a capability of feeding nearly 70 people. The development of mechanisation made a major impact up to 1960, and thereafter improved crop varieties, and chemical fertilisers and pesticides, were the main factors in the much improved levels of output and productivity. As pointed out by Dennis Avery, Director of the Hudson Institute (Avery, 1991), the impact of science-based agriculture since 1960 has been:

- a doubling of the calories of food produced;
- an increase in food supplies per capita by more than 25% in the developing world;
- an increase in food production in the developing world of 3% per annum against a population growth of 2% per annum;
- severe hunger now affecting less than 5% of the world's population in years when Africa does not have a major drought.

Figure 7.1
Future of agriculture

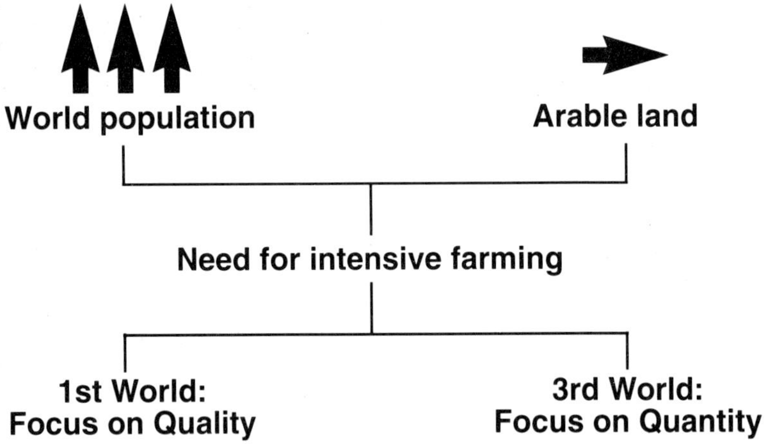

Source: Ciba Agriculture

All of this has been achieved with little increase in the area of land used; and were we trying to achieve today's level of production without today's science-based agriculture, we would need to plough up another 10 million square miles (roughly the size of the United States of America) which, even if possible, would be disastrous in conservation terms. Furthermore, whilst soil erosion has reduced in the developed world, it has increased in the developing countries due to the extension of low yield agriculture on to areas of unsuitable land.

So much for the past - let us now consider the prospects for continuing these gains in the future, when constraints are not likely to

Figure 7.2
How many consumers does a European farmer feed?

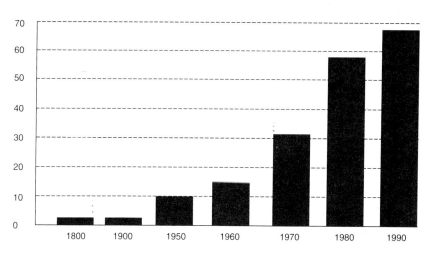

Source: Ciba Agriculture

be governed by natural resources, but by investment. If countries such as Finland and Saudi Arabia can produce surpluses of food, there are very few countries and very few situations where, given the application of scientific developments, the production of food cannot meet the requirements of population levels of the future. In my view, science has the potential to get the breakthroughs necessary to meet the needs, although it will require politicians to provide a consistent long-term framework and support. If we look at some of the existing European regulations - for example the Water Directive, and equally worrying the proposed 'use reduction' programme for pesticides, there is reason for misgivings about the political direction. There is also evidence that the UK Government, whilst generally supportive of scientific development, takes short term views on research (as pointed out by Professor Lewis in his Bawden Lecture paper) (Lewis, 1994). We need to recognise the special case of minor crops where the economics of developing and registering new ('safer') pesticides does not add up. If we do not take special measures, then either certain minor crops will no longer be grown, or better alternative treatments which could have been developed, will not be available.

Let us, however, take a positive outlook at the likely scientific developments:

- new high yielding crop varieties;
- hybrid cereals;
- precision farming utilising satellites - to monitor individual parts of field performance in terms of yield;
- new chemistry offering much reduced risks with increased benefits - a continuation of existing trends;
- seed treatment;
- diagnostics;
- biotechnology - in all its forms. (It is essential that the scientific world directs itself to increasing education of the public at large, as well as the legislators, on the benefits and risks of the development and application of biotechnological techniques).

My conclusion is that we can be optimistic that science will provide the answers and enable mankind to feed itself in a 'sustainable' manner. It depends on science and not on emotion-based regulations, and an adequate return for risk and investment. There is furthermore an urgent need for patent extension to be granted within Europe to reflect the long development time of a pesticide.

'Sustainability' is a much used word with many different definitions. To me, in the area of agriculture, it means the feeding of the current population using systems of production in such a way that future generations will also be able to satisfy their needs for food. It does not mean ensuring that exactly the same forms of flora and fauna will carry forward, since evolution - the survival of the fittest - is the most fundamental law of nature and no generation has, or ever will in the broadest sense, experience the same environment. If one accepts the definition of sustainable agriculture, then to a large extent we already have sustainable agriculture in the UK and in most of Western Europe. That is not to say, however, that we should not continue to seek improvements and continue to develop Integrated Crop Management and Integrated Pest Management as the accepted ways forward, recognising of course that these approaches are not being proposed because the present methods are not sustainable, but because they optimise the use of pesticides at the appropriate time in the appropriate economic environment that will face future generations.

I would finally like to comment briefly on some of the other issues raised earlier in this conference.

THE COMMON AGRICULTURAL POLICY

Commissioner Steichen in presenting his paper said that basically only minor changes are needed to the Common Agricultural Policy (CAP). I do not, however, accept that a continuation of the CAP in its current heavily centralised form will cope with, or be appropriate to, the changes we are going to experience over the next twenty to thirty years. Essentially, we need an approach which clearly differentiates between payments made for social purposes and those made for agronomic purposes. Furthermore, we need to move continuously towards a more open trading policy with the rest of the world. Most important though, is the need for a greater degree of local decentralised control - no centralised system can appropriately deal with an agriculture as diverse as that of Greece, Finland, Germany and Spain. If we look to the addition of the former Eastern Bloc countries in years to come, then I believe the existing CAP approach just could not cope and would inevitably collapse.

World grain stock levels have fallen significantly in recent years and currently stand at about 60 days. Given this and the additional pressure brought about by the huge projected population increase, world grain prices seem certain to rise over the coming years, and certainly within ten years the Set-aside programme will be seen as irrelevant and inappropriate to mankind's needs.

On a different aspect, reference has been made to the fact that only 1% of the CAP budget relates to environmental initiatives. Whilst this may well be true, it is only a small part of the total expenditure by those involved in agriculture, and in particular by companies in the agrochemicals sector, that goes towards protecting the environment. For example, it costs between £30 and £50 million to develop a new pesticide, of which two thirds of the expenditure relates to aspects of safety or environment. Individual farmers also spend large sums of money on tree planting, ponds and new hedgerows every year. It is therefore important that the general public does not get the impression that only small sums of money are spent within agriculture on environmental conservation - it is simply not the case.

EASTERN EUROPE

The implications of the enlargement of the European Union (EU) have been commented on by a number of speakers today. My view is that the current state of agriculture across Eastern Europe is in general very bad, and is in fact considerably worse than before the 'Wall' came down, with much lower production, a near breakdown of distribution systems in many places, and large-scale waste post production. This should be a matter of considerable concern, but it seems to be largely disregarded by the EU governments. The problem needs addressing urgently, even though it is politically uncomfortable. We seem to be truly in an 'unsustainable' state at present.

CONCLUSIONS

Looking to the future, the plea from the sector of the agricultural industry whose interests I am endeavouring to represent, is that whilst it is possible that we will, through the application of science and technology, have the potential ability to feed the massive world population forecast for thirty years hence, the open question remains - 'do we have the political will and long-term farsightedness to do so?'

Only science-based agriculture has the prospect to feed the projected world population - emotion has simply no chance and is already damaging our prospects of doing so.

REFERENCES

Anderson, J (1994) *Food and agriculture - a global perspective.* London: World Bank.

Avery, D (1991) *We don't HAVE to choose between people and wildlife.* Indianapolis: Dow Elanco Science Banquet.

Lewis, T (1994) *Commitment to long term agricultural research - a message for science, sponsors and industry.* Bawden lecture, Brighton Conference - Pests and Diseases, 1994.

Marshall BJ & Miller FA (Eds)(1995) *Priorities for a new century - agriculture, food and rural policies in the European Union.* CAS Paper 31. Reading: Centre for Agricultural Strategy.

8 Pressures on the CAP and an analysis of the way forward

Michael Franklin

My task is a dual one this afternoon - to comment on the papers so far and to say something about our study of European agricultural policy. As a member of Chatham House let me take the opportunity of saying how happy we were to collaborate with the Centre in this conference. I should also like to congratulate the organisers of this event for bringing together such an excellent array of speakers and papers.

Here at Chatham House we have been engaged in a project under the European Programme on the future direction of European agriculture (Franklin & Ockenden, 1994). It fits in extremely well with your deliberations and I am very grateful to a number of people here who have been helping us. Our study has not been as wide-ranging as today's conference. We have not attempted to cover the world scene in the way that Mr Taylor has just done and Professor Anderson did earlier this morning. I just make the point that if it is true, as Professor Anderson was saying, that over the next twenty years or so there are going to be really major opportunities for European agriculture to export, that will make the task of shifting the weight of politics, as I believe we have to, that much easier. There will of course be the temptation, which some will find irresistible, to use it as an excuse for not making the changes, but all experience suggests that structural shifts are very much more easily achieved at a time of economic development and growth than they are in a time of recession. Our time focus is slightly shorter than yours. You have taken us well into the next millennium, whereas we will be looking rather more at the period up to the end of this one. Our study is heavily policy orientated.

Finally, we have tried very hard not to be too Anglo-Saxon as befits an Institute of International Affairs. We are trying to look at issues from a European vantage point. It is true, as speakers have said today, that the UK is well ahead in the thinking process. That carries the risk that we should absorb UK thinking and ignore thinking elsewhere in the European Union (EU). But we have done a certain amount of analysis of attitudes in the rest of the EU. I would tend to confirm the view that Mr Waldegrave expressed, that there is a shift in opinion. Nobody should underestimate the fact that, as part of the MacSharry Reforms, Germany accepted the lowering of cereal prices. Historically, high cereal prices have been an absolutely vital ingredient in Germany's agriculture policy. There is no doubt that in France a major debate is going on. There are differences of view, but some strands of thinking accord very closely with the conclusions that are emerging from our studies. Nor must we forget that there is quite a legacy of feeling in the southern Member States that the Common Agricultural Policy (CAP) has operated primarily to the benefit of the northern Member States. You may find this surprising because we tend to have the opposite view. But the feeling exists and I think it is not going to disappear as a result of the changes currently in prospect.

We started our study by revisiting the objectives. I am not talking about renegotiating Article 39. That might be a waste of time. It is, however, quite important to recognise that since the CAP was first conceived priorities have changed. For instance, the importance of food security has clearly diminished. On the other hand, the environmental concerns that find no mention in Article 39 undoubtedly have grown in importance. If one were writing Article 39 now they clearly would have been included. We have found it useful to start by re-examining just what the objectives of policy are. Some of them are much more implicit than explicit; some of them are wrapped in the ambiguity which politicians find convenient. But if one is trying to think where we should be going, it is important to tease out just what the objectives of policy are in this day and age. They are undoubtedly different from those of 20 years ago. Until you have asked yourself the right questions about what you are trying to achieve you are unlikely to get the right policy mix. The bigger condemnation of the CAP is that it has not even delivered efficiently the objectives its authors had in mind.

We took as our method of working an analysis of the different pressures both internal and external, that are likely to bear on European agriculture over the next few years. Internally, we have spent quite a time looking at environmental issues. Martin Holdgate's paper gave an extremely good view of that perspective. Again I think it is probably true that the debate is further advanced and that pressures are greater in the UK than in other parts of the Union. At the beginning of his paper Martin Holdgate very usefully distinguished the apparent strands in the environmental debate, ranging from the risks and dangers of pollution to the preservation of the landscape. Each raises different issues. Some must be dealt with if degradation is to be avoided; others one would regard as coming into the area of choice. Similarly some need to be dealt with on a Community basis, whereas others, where there is no risk of distortion of competition, can be left to national or regional discretion. No problem arises, for example, if Governments decide that they want to preserve a particular kind of rural landscape. So there is scope for subsidiarity. Indeed there is a necessity for it, given the range of conditions and circumstances in the different parts of the existing Community. These differences will be even greater next year, when Finland and Austria, with their very strong emphasis on remote and difficult areas, enter the EU.

As regards the reform process itself one might have concluded from the presentation given by Mr Steichen, that following the 1992 CAP reforms, very little more needs to be done. That is not our view. We are more likely to say that the MacSharry reforms broke the mould of the CAP but left Europe with a 'dogs breakfast' if you will allow the mixed metaphor. It broke the mould because it did introduce for the first time the notion that you could bring down the price level; you didn't need to rely on price support and instead introduced direct income payments. But the new concepts applied essentially only to cereals and many commodities were left unreformed. New distortions were created, for example in the relative price level of cereals and sugar. So we would certainly take the view that what has happened so far opened up new possibilities and pushed the CAP in new and more promising directions but that there is still a great deal more to do.

Externally, the Union faces the task of implementing the GATT agreement, a task which marches hand in hand with the implementation of the MacSharry reforms. Our analysis will confirm the prevailing view that because the Union negotiated rather too well, the changes that the Uruguay Round Agreement requires can be largely accommodated within the reforms on which the Union has already agreed. However, there is a real question about how quickly the Community will run into the need for further restraint on cereals production. The assumption by the Commission that, as a result of the changes, the rate of growth in yield will slow down significantly is perhaps questionable. I don't want to imply in any way that we feel that the GATT agreement is unimportant. On the contrary, you have only to ask yourself what would happen if, as hopefully now seems unlikely as a result of the deal with Senator Dole, the US were not to ratify the GATT agreement. I don't suggest in any way the Union would go back on the MacSharry reforms. But if what I would describe as the corset of the GATT were not there, the pressures to ease the lot of the farming community would be much less readily resisted. It is also important to recall that in a few years' time there is to be a review of the Uruguay Round settlement. I don't entirely share the view that the pressures for further liberalisation will be irresistible, but I think it is well for the Community to be putting itself in a strong position to negotiate next time round.

Finally, we have naturally taken a hard look at developments in Central and Eastern Europe. That has been a dominant theme today, and rightly so. Our appreciation will accord quite closely with the rather gloomy views of both Mr Taylor and Commissioner Steichen. I noted that the Commissioner thought fifteen years was the kind of time-scale for agriculture in Central and Eastern Europe to regenerate and begin to exploit its full potential. For this reason I believe that the various financial estimates which have been made should be treated with great caution. They generally assume both that Eastern Europe will have developed and that the CAP remains unchanged, but neither assumption is realistic. One is tempted to suggest that there is a certain amount of scaremongering involved in putting such high figures forward.

Our conclusion is that, while the prospect of enlargement will and should cast its shadow forward in determining changes within the CAP, it would be unwise to suggest, as the House of Lords recent report did, that it will make those changes absolutely inevitable. I think the time-scale makes that view an incorrect one.

In the light of this analysis we identify a number of issues which are going to have to be addressed. The level of price support is the key one. It was the key which unlocked the Union's position in the GATT. There is little doubt that running the CAP at such high levels of price support has been the main culprit in creating environmental degradation. Indeed it could be said to be the root of all evil. It has created the surpluses; it has put the Union in an extremely difficult international trading position; and of course it has led to the escalating costs of the CAP.

The level of support prices is thus the central issue which has to be addressed. There is a strong case for matching what has happened on cereals with a similar programme of price reduction in the other sectors of the CAP. That of course will leave, as with cereals, a problem over income support and I think one has to accept that some degree of compensation will be necessary to gain political agreement. But it need not necessarily take the same form as last time. Hopefully there will be greater clarity as to what exactly the purpose is. Is it to compensate for lost expectations? Is it to compensate for lost asset value? Is it to maintain farm income in perpetuity? In deciding on direct payments for cereals, these questions were left unresolved. As most speakers have said today, for a whole variety of reasons any future payments need to be fully de-coupled from farming production decisions. Once payments of this kind are de-coupled, it becomes possible to allow flexibility in the way member states give or apply aid. I recognise that there are dangers of the kind which worry the National Farmers' Union in this country, for understandable reasons. The British Treasury is not notably the most generous funder in the EU. Nevertheless, de-coupling does seem to be a vital ingredient in the future.

I must pay tribute to David Naish for having been the first speaker today to tackle the whole question of supply and management. As he himself recognised, farmers tend to favour these rather cosy arrangements, at least those farmers who enjoy the benefits of a quota. But that should not disguise the fact that supply management carries with it very substantial economic costs. Mr Waldegrave quoted a fellow Minister of Agriculture as seeing nothing wrong with the sugar regime because it does not involve much cost on the Community budget. However this totally ignores the fact that, by a clever combination of arrangements, the whole of the burden of supporting a high sugar price is borne by the sugar consumer. So I think that issue does need to be addressed. And remember that the MacSharry reforms, far from introducing a greater degree of liberalisation, actually increased the amount of supply management in the system. Set-aside is another form of supply control. Its demerits have been widely recognised. It has no place in the long-term future of the CAP.

We have also been looking at some of the structural policies. They have been the poor relation of the CAP. Nevertheless, quite a lot of effort and time has gone into creating assistance schemes for the improvement of farm structure. It may well be that, for the countries that have been members of the Community a very long time, these schemes have achieved all that they can achieve. On the other hand, there may be a case for keeping them in countries like Spain and Portugal where there is still the possibility of significantly improving agricultural structure. Certainly there is a case for looking at the requirements of Central and Eastern Europe in any pre-accession strategy. There is also a case for looking at whether structural assistance should be uniquely given to farming, or whether it should not be made available to encourage other rural activities which contribute to a viable rural community. We also think there is a case for re-visiting the Less Favoured Areas scheme, if only because it has now been extended so widely in the Community. It is manifestly no longer a scheme simply to deal with rather isolated and extremely difficult areas. It has really become a vehicle for ensuring some degree of support for the viability of large rural areas.

This brings me to the wider question of rural development, again a very poor relation currently as compared with the CAP. It may surprise you to know that Commissioner Steichen is not only the Commissioner for Agriculture, but also the Commissioner for Rural Development. It is not my impression that the latter part of his title takes up very much of his time, but I believe it should do. I believe, as do many other people, that if the objectives of the Union and most Member States are now more clearly seen to be the maintenance of the rural economy rather than that of simply producing food, then the emphasis of policy, including the structural policies, should shift substantially away from agricultural policy to a more integrated approach where the maintenance of farm income will no doubt be one, but not the only, consideration.

The last area which we have examined in the Chatham House study - and it is one of considerable sensitivity - is the question of the budgetary arrangements within the Community. The MacSharry reform shifted some of the burden of support from the consumer to the tax-payer. In my view this was a desirable shift, but nevertheless it has created additional strains on the budget. If a similar process were envisaged for other sectors, that would similarly increase the budgetary costs. The question would undoubtedly arise whether compensation need all be borne on the Community budget or could be borne in some degree by Member States in support of their own national or regional policies. Of course there are dangers of distortion of competition, and strict controls would therefore be necessary. Nevertheless, it seems to us to be an area which opens up new possibilities. Once you have shifted away from price support where common financing in support of the single market is justified, to a more varied range of policies in support of the rural economy, then common financing is no longer essential or possibly even desirable.

One concluding remark. We see a great many virtues in a multi-annual programme of reform. When I was working in the Commission in the 1970s, the notion that you could decide anything for more than twelve months was laughed out of court. One thing that the GATT settlement and the MacSharry reforms have done is to create a programme of adjustment. Over several years such a programme, which is not only implemented over several years but announced in advance, has several advantages. It allows the adjustment to take place with lower cost. It introduces a degree of certainty for investment decision both for farmers and for the agri-business industry. Above all I think it is very important in the context of the political integration of the countries in Central and Eastern Europe. If that is to be achieved effectively, there must be a gradual convergence of policies so that by the time membership becomes a real possibility, there is a set of common policies in existence which makes sense for the wider Community and which would be politically and financially acceptable. On a barometric scale of reform, of which Mr Waldegrave represented today one extreme and Mr Steichen the other, our recommendations from the Chatham House study are likely to be closer to the reformist end of the spectrum. But never under-estimate the forces of inertia!

REFERENCE

Franklin, M & Ockenden, J (1994) *European agricultural policy - ten steps in the right direction.* Briefing Paper No 14. London: The Royal Institute of International Affairs.

GENERAL DISCUSSION

Mrs Vera Chaney (Green Network) expressed the view that support should not be for farmers or for the environment *(per se)* - it should be for farmers who actually demonstrate concern for the environment. She also referred to partnerships between farmers and consumers, and predicted that should partnerships be entered into with the food-processing industry, the outcome could be price reductions to the farmers and price increases for the consumers. Mrs Chaney considered also that encouragement should be given to the inclusion of 'cooking' in the educational syllabus and urged that farming organisations should give their support.

Sir David Naish in reply said that he fully favoured meaningful and beneficial partnerships between farmers and the 'food chain' comprising processors, manufacturers, retailers, and caterers, with particular recognition of the needs of consumers; he also referred to the importance of the production and provision of food at prices affordable to the consumers; and welcomed the decision of educationalists to re-introduce 'domestic science' into the national curriculum as an important development for which the NFU has been campaigning.

Mr Chris Bouchier (Agricultural Development and Advisory Service (ADAS)) referred to comments made in previous papers about the prospects of commodity output values reducing to world market levels and the impact such changes may have on agricultural asset values, especially land; he then questioned the nature of the measures that may need to be put in place to ensure the commercial viability of the industry in the event of such a major transformation.

Dr Michael Davenport in response said that he could envisage a wide range of de-coupling schemes with at one extreme one-off payments to farmers which may vary from country to country (possibly some form of unemployment benefit); at the other end of the scale Set-aside which is a 'semi-type' of decoupling (related to various environmental and non-agricultural activities); and various other possibilities in between.

Sir David Naish added that the balance sheet is extremely complex because so much of farmers' income is already from non-farming sources and he felt that the proportion is likely to move increasingly in that direction.

Ms Annabel Holt (Annabel's Crusade for the Environment) expressed concern about the possible risks and problems associated with the development of biotechnologies, and strongly urged that there can be no necessity or justification for the use of techniques relating to genetically-modified organisms.

Sir David Naish stressed that in his earlier references to this subject he had been careful to emphasise that the scientific and commercial developments of biotechnology, biodiversity, and genetic engineering cannot be ignored in this competitive world, but those in the food production and processing businesses must make every effort to satisfy themselves of the benefits and/or risks of these developments and have regard also to understanding on the part of the consumer. He therefore felt that there is every advantage in wide-ranging and open debate of all the relevant issues so that those directly concerned can reach informed assessments of the balance between risks and benefits.

Mrs Mary Smith (Farmer) referred to the comments made by Sir David Naish about the desirability of reducing the number of grant aid schemes, and stressed the need for improved technical communication with farmers, especially where tree planting and environmental developments are proposed on agricultural land.

Sir David Naish accepted this point and added his concern that because of the number and complexity of schemes, some farmers are not making the most effective use of available funding. He therefore favoured a simpler and generally available system, providing support towards the cost of agricultural/environmental improvements, administered on a 'menu' basis.

Dr John Slater (Ministry of Agriculture, Fisheries and Food) referred to the recently issued European Commission report entitled *EC Agricultural Policy into the 21st century* and strongly recommended study of the comments relating to the separation of policies into those that achieved farming efficiency and productivity and those that relate to rural and environmental objectives. He also referred to the high estimates of cost in the report, of applying the CAP to the Central and Eastern European (CEE) countries and commented that whilst estimates prepared by MAFF were lower, they were nevertheless significant.

Sir Michael Franklin agreed that the EC Report is relevant and well worth reading provided account is taken of the reasons for the long delay in publication. On the question of estimates of cost, he was concerned that these may lead some people to the conclusion that accession of the CEE countries may be politically and financially impossible. He felt that such a view would be profoundly mistaken and urged that the estimates should not be misinterpreted or misused.

Mr Hugh Oliver-Bellasis (Farmer) said that he felt he must challenge Mr Don Taylor's statement that agriculture is currently fully sustainable, on the ground that a large body of data shows that the number of beneficial insects is being reduced significantly by the use of broad-spectrum insecticides. He accordingly felt that the agrochemicals industry has a responsibility to ensure that the regulatory process is based on up-to-date parameters which take account of the current state of knowledge.

Mr Don Taylor's response was that he had expressed his personal view that to a large extent we already have a 'sustainable' agriculture in the UK and in most of western Europe. On the question of the regulatory procedures he said that in seeking approval of the safety and efficacy of proposed new products, the data submitted by the agrochemicals industry to the appropriate regulatory authorities is closely examined and discussed over a period of about two years, and he was therefore confident that current knowledge and scientific developments are taken properly into account.

Marshall BJ & Miller FA (Eds)(1995) *Priorities for a new century - agriculture, food and rural policies in the European Union.* CAS Paper 31. Reading: Centre for Agricultural Strategy.

Summary and Conclusions

John Marsh

The programme suggests that I am to provide a summary of the papers and discussions which have contributed to this conference. You will be relieved that I have no intention of attempting to recapitulate all we have heard. Rather I wish to take the opportunity to thank a number of people and organisations and to indulge myself by highlighting some of the important themes which have surfaced.

We are very grateful to our Chairmen, Sir William Benyon and Mrs Teresa Wickham who have managed the business of this complex day so well that we reached its conclusion on time and in good order. We appreciate the support of our sponsors, whose generosity made it possible to organise this meeting - their names appear on the programme as 'Supporting Organisations'. I am glad to reinforce the thanks already expressed by our chairmen to our distinguished speakers, whose papers have drawn our attention to many of the issues which confront agriculture and its policy makers as they prepare for the coming century. Finally, I must thank our CAS conference team who have worked tirelessly over many months to ensure that this conference has run in a smooth and workmanlike way.

The first highlight I would stress is the inevitably of change. Virtually all the papers reminded us that we live in a world which has to cope with population growth, with changes in the level and distribution of real incomes and in the techniques of production and communication. We also live on the threshold of changes stemming from the further enlargement of the European Union (EU) to the East. Out attitudes too are changing. We have become more attached to markets and less confident of the ability of policies to solve our problems. That must have important implications for farmers. It would be foolish in a world shaped by these powerful forces to become complacent about food security. Equally, we should be encouraged that all the papers we have listened to envisaged the possibility of good outcomes in sharp contrast to the gloomy predictions which often emerge from such discussions.

A second highlight is that we, ourselves, have to be prepared to change if we are to seize the opportunity for good outcomes. There is a need for new thinking about our industry, about the policies we have in place and even about our lifestyles. That process needs to begin now. The task is to build upon achievements of the past not to dismantle them.

In deciding how to respond we have some very important assets at our disposal. We need much more understanding of the physical, social and economic world in which we live but we have, and must seek to preserve, a strong science base. We have industries on and off the farm which are capable of turning that science into action. We have many innovative and entrepreneurial farmers. Producers of fertilisers, pesticides and herbicides and of farm machinery are able to equip modern farmers with powerful tools to meet both market and environmental requirements. Our food manufacturing sector translates the outputs of farming into a huge variety of products to nourish and entertain the consumer whilst our retail sector is better equipped than ever before to detect and reflect the preferences of consumers to the producers.These are important assets although making full use of them may involve uncomfortable pressures for many within and beyond the sector.

There are, too, some worrying obstacles to a process of successful development. Much of our debate takes place in compartments and too often we conduct separate dialogues about the problems of farmers, of the environment, of the rural economy, of trade, and of welfare without recognising their interaction. There are some welcome signs of change in this. The government's promised 'Rural White Paper' is clearly to be interdepartmental. In Brussels, however, DG VI still seems to resent others interfering in its agricultural domain. This does not match the needs of the world of the 21st century with its information superhighways and growing global awareness that policy decisions in any one sector have implications for the rest of society.

A further obstacle is the extent to which present policies entrench the interests of their clients. Because of the way in which farm support is delivered it is extremely difficult to cope at one and the same time with the need for greater competitiveness and the social and environmental goals of agricultural policy. I was disappointed by what the Commissioner had to say about the need for further modification of the

CAP. This imposes costs on the EU not only in a financial sense but in terms of wasted natural and human resources. Such costs weaken our ability to cope with the challenges spelled out in the papers to which we have listened.

Perhaps the worst of our problems is complacency. This may be based on a misguided belief that we have 'solved' our problems, that we have survived past scares and that, if we leave it alone, science or government will sort out our problems. The effects of this can be intensified if there is a belief that we can make progress without effort, without thought, or without a willingness to question present practice on the part of each one of us.

Among those who are not complacent there is often a cry for 'a strategy for the industry'. That should be good news for a Centre for Agricultural Strategy but there are some uncomfortable realities which have to be faced. If what is meant by a 'strategy' is the application of a blueprint, from Brussels or from London, that would give each of the actors instructions about what was to be done in the future, the outcome is likely to be damaging, costly and infeasible. Devising a strategy is not an activity for 'other' people but for everyone who is engaged in the industry. Certainly it involves Brussels but equally it demands thought on the part of each individual farmer. Each 'actor' has to accept that in an uncertain world there are no simple answers. Each business has to take responsibility for assessing risks and opportunities affecting its enterprise and for charting a course which will enable it to operate to best advantage. At all levels this implies a willingness to listen, to learn, to adapt and to take risks.

This conference was called to assist that process. None of us expected to depart with all the problems resolved, still less with a new set of instructions about how to conduct our business. What we have done is to question some common assumptions, possibly to raise some hopes, and to recognise that the next fifty years will not simply be a re-run of the half-century which has just passed. If we are to be well placed to shape that future and to equip those who are to live in it to cope satisfactorily with its opportunities and challenges, we need to discuss these issues now. As I see it this is one of the key roles of our Centre. We shall seek to encourage similar debates and to visit other relevant themes. We believe this is a constructive and important activity and we are grateful to all who have made it possible - our sponsors, speakers and, of course, all of you who have listened with patience and contributed with vigour throughout a long but fascinating day.

Appendix
List of Authors

Professor Jock Anderson; Agricultural Technology Adviser, Agriculture and Natural Resources Department, The World Bank, 1818 H Street, NW, Washington DC 20433

Dr Michael Davenport; Consultant and Research Associate to Overseas Development Institute, 24 Norfolk Mansions, Prince of Wales Drive, London SW11 4HJ

Sir Michael Franklin KCB; Chairman, European Programme, The Royal Institute of International Affairs, Chatham House, 10 St. James's Square, London SW1Y 4LE

Sir Martin Holdgate CB; formerly Director General, International Union for the Conservation of Nature and Natural Resources, 35 Wingate Way, Trumpington, Cambridge CB2 2HD

Mr Martin Lowe; President, United Kingdom Agricultural Supply Trade Association Ltd; Managing Director, Intermol, Knowle Hill Park, Fairmile Lane, Cobham, Surrey KT11 2PD

Professor John Marsh CBE; Department of Agricultural Economics and Management, University of Reading and Director of the Centre for Agricultural Strategy, 1 Earley Gate, Reading, Berkshire RG6 2AT

Sir David Naish DL; President, National Farmers' Union, 22 Long Acre, London WC2E 9LY

M René Steichen; Member of the Commission of the European Communities, Rue de la Loi - 200, B - 1049 Brussels

Mr Don Taylor; Chairman, British Agrochemicals Association Ltd; Managing Director, Ciba Agriculture, Whittlesford, Cambridge CB2 4QT

115

Chairmen

Morning Sessions

Sir William Benyon DL; Chairman of Advisory Committee, Centre for Agricultural Strategy, University of Reading.

Afternoon Sessions

Mrs Teresa Wickham, Member of Advisory Commitee, Centre for Agricultural Strategy, University of Reading.

Centre for Agricultural Strategy

Sponsorship Scheme

The Centre gratefully acknowledges the long-term support under this scheme of the following organisations:

DowElanco Europe

The Englefield Charitable Trust

The Ernest Cook Trust

Zeneca Agrochemicals

Centre Publications

Reports

1 *Land for agriculture* (1976) £1.50.
2 *Phosphorus: a source for UK agriculture* (1978) £1.75.
3 *Capital for agriculture* (1978)‡
4 *Strategy for the UK dairy industry* (1978) £2.95.
5 *National food policy in the UK* (1979) £2.85.
6 *Strategy for the UK forest industry* (1980)‡
7 *The efficiency of British Agriculture* (1980) £2.85.
8 Jollans, JL (Ed) (1985) *The teaching of agricultural marketing in the UK* £6.00.
9 Jollans, JL (1985) *Fertilisers in UK farming* £8.00.
10 Craig, GM, Jollans, JL & Korbey, A (Eds) (1986) *The case for agriculture: an independent assessment* £9.50.
11 Carruthers, SP (Ed) (1986) *Alternative enterprises for agriculture in the UK*‡
12 Carruthers, SP (Ed) (1986) *Land use alternatives for UK agriculture* £3.00.
13 Harrison, Alan & Tranter, RB (1989) *The changing financial structure of farming* £8.75.
14 Harrison, Alan & Tranter, RB (1994) *The recession and farming: crisis or readjustment?* £8.50.
15 Carruthers, SP, Miller, FA & Vaughan, CMA (1994) *Crops for industry and energy.* &18.50

Papers

1 Marsh, JS (1977) *UK agricultural policy within the European Community* £1.50.
2 Tranter, RB (Ed) (1978) *The future of upland Britain* Proceedings of a symposium organised by CAS in conjunction with the Department of Agriculture and Horticulture, 19-22 September 1977‡

3 Harrison, A, Tranter, RB & Gibbs, RS (1977) *Landownership by public and semi-public institutions in the UK* £1.75.

4 Collins, EJT (1978) *The economy of upland Britain, 1750-1950: an illustrated review* £2.20.

5 McCalla, AF (1978) *International agricultural research: potential impact on world food markets and on UK agricultural strategy‡*

6 Swinbank, A (1978) *The British interest and the green pound‡*

7 Robbins, CJ (Ed) (1978) *Food, health and farming: reports of panels on the implications for UK agriculture* £2.40.

8 Ritson, C (1980) Self-sufficiency and food security £2.00.

9 Tranter, RB (Ed) (1981) *Smallfarming and the Nation* Proceedings of a conference organised by the Smallfarmers' Association, 27 March 1980 £2.00.

10 Jollans, JL (Ed) (1981) *Grassland in the British economy* Proceedings of a symposium organised by the Department of Agriculture, the Department of Agricultural Economics and Management, the Grassland Research Institute and the Centre for Agricultural Strategy, 15-17 September 1980 £10.00.

11 Marshall, BJ & Tranter, RB (Eds) (1982) *Smallfarming and the rural community* Proceedings of a conference organised by the Smallfarmers' Association, 28 March 1981‡

12 Hallam, D (1983) *Livestock development planning: a quantitative framework‡*

13 Carruthers, SP & Jones, MR (1983) *Biofuel production strategies for UK agriculture* £6.50.

14 Jollans, JL (1983) *Agriculture and human health* Report of a study and the proceedings of a symposium, 11-13 July 1983‡

15 Tranter, RB (Ed) (1983) *Strategies for family-worked farms in the UK* Proceedings of a symposium organised by the Smallfarmers' Association and the Centre for Agricultural Strategy, 21-22 September 1983 £7.50.

16 Korbey, A (Ed) (1984) *Investing in rural harmony: a critique* Proceedings of a seminar organised by the Centre for Agricultural Strategy, 10 April 1984 £5.00.

17 Korbey, A (Ed) (1985) *Food production and our rural environment - the way ahead* Proceedings of a symposium organised by the Centre for Agricultural Strategy, 19 November 1984 £5.50.

18 Miller, FA & Tranter, RB (Eds) (1988) *Public perception of the countryside* Papers presented at a conference organised by the Centre for Agricultural Strategy as part of a study commissioned by the Countryside Foundation, 7 January 1988 £4.50.

19 Bennett, RM (Ed) (1989) *The greenhouse effect and UK agriculture* Proceedings of a conference organised by the Centre for Agricultural Strategy, 14 July 1989 £15.00.

20 Miller, FA (Ed) (1990) *Food safety in the human food chain* Proceedings of a conference organised by the Centre for Agricultural Strategy, 27 September 1989 £15.00.

21 Bather, DM & Miller, FA (1991) *Peatland utilisation in the British Isles* £2.00. (The detailed report to the Peat Producers' Association entitled 'Peatland utilisation in the UK and Ireland', on which paper 21 is based, is also available)

22 Carruthers, SP (Ed) (1991) *Farm animals: it pays to be humane* Proceedings of a conference organised by the Centre for Agricultural Strategy, 12 September 1990 £15.00.

23 Wise, TE (Ed) (1991) *Agricultural and food research - who benefits?* Proceedings of a conference organised by the Centre for Agricultural Strategy, 18 December 1990 £14.00.

24 Miller, FA (Ed) (1991) *Agricultural policy and the environment* Proceedings of a conference organised by the Centre for Agricultural Strategy, 7 June 1991 £13.50.

25 Marshall, BJ (Ed) (1992) *Sustainable livestock farming into the 21st Century* Proceedings of a conference organised by the Centre for Agricultural Strategy, 12 September 1991 £15.50.

26 CAS (1992) *Strategies for the rural economy* Proceedings of a conference organised by the Centre for Agricultural Strategy, 30 June 1992 £30.00.

27 Miller, FA (Ed) (1993) *Eastern Europe: opportunities and needs for food and agriculture* Proceedings of a conference organised by the Centre for Agricultural Strategy, 17 September 1992 £19.50.

28 Carruthers, SP (Ed) (1994) *Crisis on the family farm: ethics or economics?* Proceedings of a conference organised by the Centre for Agricultural Strategy, 30 March 1993. In preparation.

29 Marshall, BJ & Miller FA (Eds) (1994) *Water services and agriculture: key issues and strategic options* Proceedings of a conference organised by the Centre for Agricultural Strategy, 14 December 1993. £20.00.

30 Ansell, DJ & Vincent, SA (1994) *An evaluation of set-aside management in the European Union* with special reference to Denmark, France, Germany and the UK £22.50.

31 Marshall, BJ & Miller FA (Eds) (1995) *Priorities for a new century - agriculture, food and rural policies in the European Union* Proceedings of a conference organised by the Centre for Agricultural Strategy, 24 November 1994. £20.00.

32 Jones, PJ, Rehman, T, Harvey, DR, Tranter, RB, Marsh, JS, Bunce, RGH, & Howard, DC (1995) *Developing LUAM (Land Use Allocation Model) and modelling CAP reforms* £16.50.

‡ Out of print but available in facsimile

Joint Publications

2 Choe, ZR (1986) *A Strategy for pasture improvement by smallfarmers in upland Korea* Published in collaboration with Gyeonsang National University, Korea £10.00.

3 Ansell, DJ & Done, JT (1988) *Veterinary research and development: cost benefit studies on products for the control of animal diseases* Published jointly with the British Veterinary Association £5.00.

4   Ansell, DJ & Tranter, RB (1992) *Set-aside; in theory and in practice* Published jointly with the Department of Agricultural Economics and Management, University of Reading   £14.50.

Mailing List
To receive invoiced copies of all future publications please ask to be put on the mailing list.
Standing Orders
To receive invoiced copies of all future publications please ask to be put on the standing order list.
Orders
From: The Centre for Agricultural Strategy, University of Reading, 1 Earley Gate, Reading RG6 2AT. Telephone: (01734) 318152. Prices include postage. Please make cheques payable to 'The University of Reading'. We cannot accept payment by 'BACS'.